The New Planetary Reality

THE COMING AVATĀRA

& THE NINE PATHS TO ENLIGHTENMENT

IMRE VALLYON

The New Planetary Reality
The Coming Avatāra & The Nine Paths to Enlightenment
by Imre Vallyon

ISBN 978-0-909038-65-6
First Edition: June 2012

Sounding-Light Publishing Ltd
PO Box 771, Hamilton 3240, New Zealand
www.soundinglight.com

CONTENTS

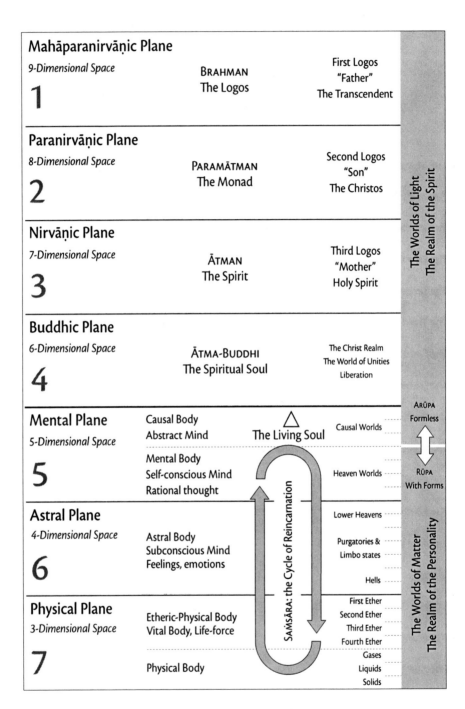

Mahāparanirvāṇic Plane 9-Dimensional Space **1**		BRAHMAN The Logos	First Logos "Father" The Transcendent	
Paranirvāṇic Plane 8-Dimensional Space **2**		PARAMĀTMAN The Monad	Second Logos "Son" The Christos	The Worlds of Light The Realm of the Spirit
Nirvāṇic Plane 7-Dimensional Space **3**		ĀTMAN The Spirit	Third Logos "Mother" Holy Spirit	
Buddhic Plane 6-Dimensional Space **4**		ĀTMA-BUDDHI The Spiritual Soul	The Christ Realm The World of Unities Liberation	

ARŪPA
Formless

Mental Plane 5-Dimensional Space **5**	Causal Body Abstract Mind Mental Body Self-conscious Mind Rational thought	△ The Living Soul	Causal Worlds Heaven Worlds	RŪPA With Forms

Astral Plane 4-Dimensional Space **6**	Astral Body Subconscious Mind Feelings, emotions		Lower Heavens Purgatories & Limbo states Hells	The Worlds of Matter The Realm of the Personality
Physical Plane 3-Dimensional Space **7**	Etheric-Physical Body Vital Body, Life-force Physical Body	SAṀSĀRA: the Cycle of Reincarnation	First Ether Second Ether Third Ether Fourth Ether Gases Liquids Solids	

THE SEVEN GREAT PLANES OF BEING

THE MYSTERY OF THE
COMING AVATĀRA

The Past Avatāras

To understand the mystery of the Coming Avatāra, you first have to understand the past before you can understand what is happening now.

The Sanskrit word Avatāra means "one who is coming down"—*ava* means "down" and *tāra* means "coming" or "emerging". So an *Avatāra* is an entity that has emerged or come down from some higher realm or plane of existence. That higher realm may be the Causal World, the Buddhic World, Nirvāṇa or even the realms beyond Nirvāṇa[1]. The lowest kind of Avatāra would come from the Causal World and the highest from beyond Nirvāṇa, the latter being extremely rare in the history of our planet. Over the last 200,000 years, Avatāras have come down to teach people many times, in ancient Persia, China, Egypt, Greece and on several occasions in India.

In India, the tradition of the Avatāra has existed for the last 6,000 years, but unfortunately the concept of the Avatāra has been over-used. In the Indian tradition, somebody who has attained some level

---

[1] See the diagram *The Seven Great Planes of Being.*

of Union with God is nominated an Avatāra by his or her disciples—an Avatāra of Love or an Avatāra of Wisdom, an incarnation of the Deity. They use the word Avatāra wrongly, not in the *true* sense of somebody who descended from a higher level. There is a word for one who attains and becomes enlightened in their lifetime, JĪVANMUKTA, and there are many Yogīs and Mystics in India who are Jīvanmuktas, but unfortunately they are also called Avatāras. This confuses the issue because there are not that many Avatāras on the planet at any given time.

The principle of the Avatāra has to do with natural evolution, which is a much vaster reality than what was put forward by Darwin. Natural evolution is a cosmic force sweeping through the physical realm, motivating the Mineral Kingdom, the Plant Kingdom, the Animal Kingdom and the Human Kingdom, as well as the Elemental Kingdom and the Angelic Kingdom beyond the physical realm. Like a massive tidal wave, it slowly but steadily pushes the planet, the Solar System and the entire Galaxy forward over vast eons of time. If the evolution of human beings depended on this natural force only, we would have made some progress in consciousness and abilities, but that progress would have been infinitely slow and we would not be as we are now; we would still be rather primitive.

Because of the slowness of evolution, therefore, there are angelic hierarchies within our Solar System that oversee the evolutionary progress of the planets. These angels are the original Virgin Spirits who did not participate in the Fall, so their cosmic vision and understanding were never closed down; hence they have always been able to see the Divine Plan and have never deviated from it. Under their inspiration, a *Planetary Hierarchy* is created to speed up the evolution of each planet.

Our Planetary Hierarchy (which we also call the *Spiritual Hierarchy*) consists of great Adepts and Masters who attained the states of Christhood and Buddhahood over many thousands of years, and they form an internal hierarchy of enlightened human beings within the planet. They stimulate our evolution, as much as is lawfully possible in any given period of history, by sending down one of their messengers. You will have heard of the Buddha, the Christ, Kṛṣṇa, Rama, Lao Tzu, Quan Yin, Isis, Zoroaster, Moses and Mohammed—just a few of the many beings who have been sent to speed up the vibration of Humanity in a particular location and time. Many Gurus, Masters and Spiritual Teachers are Avatāras who have consciously incarnated from the higher realms in order to teach Humanity and help our spiritual evolution.

Historically speaking, the influence of these messengers from our Spiritual Hierarchy was conditional; they only influenced a certain localized area. They stimulated the religious, social, philosophical, scientific and cultural structures of the local community and brought a new understanding, a new impulse towards the creation of a better civilization and the renewal of that part of the planet. In actuality, the Avatāras planted the *seeds* of a new energy-wave but it was through their disciples that the new impulse slowly filtered into society and changed society over the centuries. When Christ came, nothing changed in His time. It was only through the second, third and fourth generations of Christians that the world noticed the new wave of energy. The Buddha had about four hundred disciples who travelled around and taught, but the major changes in India came after their time. It was the same with all the Avatāras: they managed to stir a few people into activity but it was their disciples who gradually spread the New Energy into society.

It is important to understand that we're talking about energies, not just a teaching or philosophical ideas. Unfortunately, people refer to what Jesus said in the Sermon on the Mount, what Moses was given in the Ten Commandments or what Lao Tzu wrote in the Tao Te Ching as if they were intellectual ideas on how to live in society. The work of the Avatāras is not just to bring down clever sayings or make rules about what people should or should not do—everybody knows that they should not kill, but they still do it anyhow. It is about real *energies*. When Christ came He brought in the powerful energy of Cosmic Love; Buddha brought in the energy of Wisdom, an incredibly bright luminous Mind-energy. Lao Tzu worked with another aspect of the Wisdom-energy. Every Avatāra came in with a specific mission to stimulate a particular race in a specific way, and it was the invisible waves of energy which they brought down with them—their amazing *energy-work*—that changed human consciousness at that time.

So, we have established that Avatāras bring down energy to change the structure of society and that it is necessary for these beings to come in order to stimulate the planetary consciousness at the time and place where they are born. The mystery of the *Coming* Avatāra, however, is very profound because it is something completely different from what has happened in the past.

Now, our planet has reached a crisis point and it is necessary for a *Planetary Avatāra* to come and help us.

The Coming Avatāra

Besides Human Avatāras, there are other, higher Avatāras: Cosmic Avatāras, great beings who have gone beyond the level of the most advanced spiritual evolution in the Cosmos; Solar Logoic Avatāras, great beings who have evolved beyond the evolutionary level of our

Solar Logos and who stimulate the initiatory process of Spiritual Suns; Interplanetary Avatāras, great beings who stimulate the interlinking between our planetary system and our Solar System; and Planetary Avatāras, great beings who embrace planetary structures and concern themselves with the spiritual evolution of planets such as our Earth.

Planetary Avatāras are not beings from our planet at all, but entities that have a high status of Cosmic Attainment, having evolved above not only the human but also the angelic and archangelic levels of evolution. In our case, the Earth Planetary Avatāra (the Coming Avatāra) is a vast Cosmic Intelligence that is able to embrace the visible and invisible dimensions of the planet—the Physical, Astral, Mental, Buddhic and Nirvāṇic Worlds—all within its own auric field, trying to help the process of planetary transformation on Earth by healing and balancing the conflicting energies pervading the invisible dimensions[2].

The Coming Avatāra has been influencing the planet since about 1875, and by "coming" we mean that it is within the auric energy-field (the invisible dimensions) of the planet and its influence will increase as it penetrates the physical dimension. In my book *Planetary Transformation*, I detailed many reasons for the rapid changes the planet has been undergoing since 1875, with the coming of this New Vibration onto the planet:

- The movement into the energy-vibration of the Aquarian Age
- Our planet undergoing a *cosmic initiation* and thereby receiving extra cosmic energies
- The initiation of our Solar Logos by another greater entity resulting in the exchange of dynamic energies

---

[2] In spiritual language we use the word *dimensions* in terms of worlds or planes of being, not the mathematical or scientific definition of *dimensions*.

- The movement of our Solar System into a new energy-reality within the Milky Way Galaxy

As you can see, many cosmic forces and energies have been increasingly stimulating the planet since 1875, but they are not the energies of the Coming Avatāra. Rather, these high-frequency energies bombarding our planet have been preparing the planet, and human consciousness, so that we can now receive an Avatāra that is *global* in nature, an Avatāra concerned with the entire planetary life rather than only the stimulation of a limited locality.

Accordingly, the New Avatāra is not going to be a person born in India, China or America; it is not coming to one nation or one religion like the Jewish Messiah (which by the way is the Hebrew word for "Avatāra"). Naturally, everybody wants the Avatāra to come from their religion. The Buddhists think that the Avatāra will come as another Buddha dressed in yellow robes; the Christians think he will come as Jesus Christ in Bethlehem; and the Muslims think he will go to Mecca and preach from the Kaaba Stone. But that will not happen. The whole planet is being stimulated and the energy-field of the Avatāra embraces every field of knowledge—science, art, politics, social science, medicine, education—anywhere there is a consciousness that can be moved. People in these fields will sense a new stimulus and feel a need to change things, and anyone can be stimulated whatever their background or life situation, provided they can tune into the New Energy.

The Avatāra has not yet fully manifested. I would say that it will probably reach full incarnation within two or three hundred years. By *incarnation* I mean embedding itself in the whole planetary structure—from the Nirvāṇic dimensions right down to the physical dimensions—so that the whole planet will be embraced within its consciousness. If the Avatāra suddenly appeared in its full blazing glory, its energy-field would be so strong that it would create even bigger problems on Earth because of the opposition from the materialistic elements of society. For thousands of years the human reaction to any new manifestation or understanding has been to reject or destroy it, so as the Avatāric influence increases, there will be massive confusion in society. Some will realize that the phenomena and the energy of change are real while others will deny them, claiming they are hallucinations or political conspiracies.

In the next one or two hundred years, or even earlier, there could be a massive clash in society between those who want to move into the New Reality with open eyes and open minds and those who want to close themselves down even more because they are afraid of the Truth. This clash could have a religious cause, because there are certain fundamentalist religious groups in the world that are back in the fourteenth century and cannot adapt to the New Vibration. They will oppose it with all their strength and weapons. Conflict will arise within families, tribes, religions, nations and societies, and people will see conflict within themselves, between the part of them that wants to go into the New Reality and the part that resists. The world could be in a huge mess.

Consequently, the New Avatāra is coming gradually and, as the pressure increases, more and more people will have the opportunity to awaken to the Spiritual Life and the Spiritual Reality, to the fact that they are spiritual beings walking on this planet.

The Masters and the Angels

The phenomenon of the Coming Avatāra will result in many Spiritual Teachers, Gurus and Masters coming into existence—some are already here now—each receiving and expressing some part of that Cosmic Avatāric Vibration. They will be the real New Age Teachers, born with the conscious awareness of what they need to do to be part of the transformation of the planet. There will be specialists like me who work on the esoteric side of things, stimulating an awareness of the Inner Knowledge on a deeper level, and Gurus who are not of the ancient traditions but who know and understand all the old traditions and teach from the here and now.

There is also a possibility of the reincarnation of some of the past Avatāras, the great Souls who were the Christ, Moses, Mohammed or Lao Tzu. They may choose to incarnate with the Coming Avatāra—*may* choose. It doesn't mean that they will do so. It will depend on whether or not it is *safe* for them to come. Throughout history Human Avatāras were opposed because their high-frequency energy stirred up society too much. The Christ was crucified because He annoyed the materialistic religious authorities of the day, and Buddhism could only survive outside of India after the death of the Buddha.

The Angelic Kingdom will also respond, and that is why it is said in the Bible that "when the Christ comes He will come with His masters and His angels" (MATTHEW 24: 30–31). The angels understand the need to change the lower inner worlds—the astral and mental dimensions—but as the energy of the Avatāra comes down, the angels will be inspired to help the physical dimension also. This is difficult for them, however, because they have two handicaps: firstly they don't have physical bodies and secondly the human beings who do have physical bodies do not respond to their attempts at communication. For example, the so-called crop circles that appear in different parts of the planet are their way of trying to communicate Cosmic Truth to us in mathematical language, which is their normal way of communicating on the Causal World. Through these geometric patterns, they try to tell us that there is more happening in the Cosmos other than just physical life on Earth.

There will also be signs and wonders in the skies as a part of the angelic manifestation, as it was prophesied in the Bible: "There will be a new Heaven and a new Earth" (REVELATION 21: 1). A few years ago I was looking up into the sky, which had some greyish clouds in it, when suddenly the scene changed and the clouds turned dynamic red, orange, blue and green. The colours moved slowly across the sky and changed shapes with the clouds. It was quite amazing. What I am trying to say is that increasingly more people will see the new sky (the new Heaven) because it will become more obvious as the New Reality unfolds.

The Human Dilemma

At present, the biggest problem for planet Earth in terms of its evolutionary plan is the human family. Why? Because humans have not developed Cosmic Vision, the ability to see *internally*. If we could see the invisible forces working throughout the planet, we would be able to cooperate with the Divine Plan and work *with* the coming changes. Every religious tradition refers to a Divine Being, an incarnation of the Deity, who is supposed to come and change the world. In Christianity it is the second coming of the Christ; in Buddhism it is the coming of Lord Maitreya; in Hinduism it is the Kalki Avatāra; and in Islam it is the Imam Mahdi. What the scriptures don't understand is: it's one thing to say that this being will come, but what happens if there are a whole lot of rebellious kids—like seven billion humans!—who don't want to be changed?

The New Planetary Avatāra will naturally have to focus special attention on human beings, in the same way that a school teacher focuses more attention on the children who are not behaving so that the whole class can function in the best way. But herein lies the tragedy of the human system: human beings were given free will and this means that according to the Cosmic Mind they are allowed to do what they want and learn from their own doing. If they do wrong, the Law will hit them; if they do right, the Law will help them. That Law of Adjustment we call Karma and it is a device to teach humans.

Free will also means that entities that are more evolved than us must not interfere in our affairs. It would be easy for the angelic hierarchies to blank out the minds of human beings and force them to start working according to the Divine Plan. But that is against the Law and is not allowed in the Cosmos. The only thing other beings can do is teach Humanity, and that is why there are Gurus, Teachers and Masters who come from time to time to help Humanity.

Similarly, the Avatāra cannot force people to change either. The Avatāra will, like all the Spiritual Teachers before, give out a certain energy stream and allow people to go with it or not. It cannot do anything more because, according to Cosmic Law, higher powers cannot control lower powers. So those who pick up that energy stream will be able to work with it and those who reject it will not. This is where the Human Avatāras, the human Teachers, come in because it is their function to *explain* what is happening. The New Avatāra doesn't explain; it just works with energy streams as a distributor of Cosmic Energy. The Spiritual Teachers are closer to Humanity than the Avatāra and it is through them that salvation will come, provided that people understand what is happening and what they are supposed be doing about it.

The Spiritual Teachers who work along this line will help you understand the real situation, the beauty, grandeur and vastness and the amazing possibilities of the Coming Avatāra, and through that understanding you can change and help the world. Your mind is actually a receiving and broadcasting mechanism. The knowledge you receive is automatically broadcast from your mind without you having to consciously think about it. As you pick up the New Vibration, the frequency of your mental body changes and that new energy-wave goes out into the world. You don't have to preach; you just have to be yourself, because that expanded understanding of yourself will be broadcast into your environment and it will help people pick up the New Vibration.

There will always be those who cannot or do not want to be stimulated, the many materialists who refuse to believe anything they cannot see, hear or touch, but there will also be many people able to sense the stimulating, high-frequency energy of the Avatāra. Everybody will have the opportunity to jump ahead of their normal rate of evolutionary development or even complete their spiritual journey and attain Causal Consciousness or even Buddhic or Nirvāṇic Consciousness—if they have the capacity to do so. It remains to be seen how many human beings will be able to change and move ahead in spiritual evolution and how many will miss the opportunity.

Human beings have the choice to cooperate with the process or not. If we do not, the suffering and the problems will continue. If we cooperate, however, we will have a Golden Age on this planet within two or three hundred years, and the planet can be turned into a field of Light because the Avatāric Energy will flood the whole Solar System with Light and increase the Light-energy on our planet a million times more than it is now.

The Merging of the Worlds

All the Avatāras of the past brought down some particular quality: the Christ brought Love, the Buddha brought Wisdom, Rama brought a tremendous sense of order and social structure in human consciousness. But the New Avatāra is a *massive field of energy* that contains all the qualities of the past Avatāras, even qualities which have never manifested before; it is a *unifying vibration* that will unite all the cosmic vibrations that have been bombarding the planet since 1875. This energy will merge together everything that is normally compartmentalized, which means that if you are able to receive the energy of the New Planetary Avatāra, your mind will no longer work in its compartmentalized way. Your ordinary mind will merge with your subconscious mind (Feminine Mind), which will merge with the Superconscious Mind (Transcendental Mind). Then humans will be able to use the powers of the subconscious mind and the Superconscious Mind, so those who are able to evolve rapidly will be completely new beings.

What is even more dramatic is that, if we are able to respond to this incredible stimulation of Cosmic Evolution, *the Physical World will merge with the Astral World.* There will literally be a new Heaven and a new Earth.

This means that human beings will be able to see the Astral World as people in the Astral World see it, and astral entities will be able to see the Physical World as we do. Normally, the Astral World and the Physical World are cut off from each other. They have to be, because the astral energies are a hundred times more powerful than physical energies and would completely obliterate the normal human consciousness. So Nature provides a safety device, a barrier that prevents human beings from being aware of the Astral World so that they can function normally in this physical dimension. (There is another barrier between the Astral World and the Causal World and between the Causal World and the Buddhic World. Each world is separated on purpose so that the entities evolving there can maintain their own identity.)

But as the Physical and Astral Worlds slowly merge over the next few hundred years, Humanity will gradually recognize the nature of the invisible worlds. Imagine how it will be for the many materialists who have never believed that there is life after death. What will they do when they are suddenly aware of another universe around them full of incredible energies? Billions of human beings will have to accept that there are other realities beyond physical existence, and that could be incredibly challenging for them. And what about the religious authorities, the same authorities who rejected Christ when He came? What will they do when the Inner Worlds open up? They will want to deny it because it will be too much for them.

The most tragic thing will be that people will not understand what is happening; psychologically, that will be devastating for many people. So the whole aim of this book is to tell people that there are invisible worlds and there always have been; that we exist as Souls, not just physical bodies; that there are major changes coming and the planet is not going to continue "sleeping" as before; and that we might see the Astral World (or "Heaven") before we die. Christians believe that if they are good they will go to Heaven after they die. But what will happen when people become aware that the incredible vastness of Heaven is already here, and they realize it not just as a religious belief but as a *reality* that can be experienced?

So it is important to understand what is coming and work with it, because what is coming is normal—normal because it is part of the Divine Plan, not something a religious authority decided to do.

It is a vast cosmic event beyond any religion, any political party, any country—beyond anything.

The new energy of the Coming Avatāra is getting stronger and stronger every year and more and more people will be tuning into this energy-field and will be able to use it. As this stimulation increases over the next two or three hundred years, we will have a completely different society than ever before, completely different than any utopia or ideal society dreamed up by writers. In other words, we have a golden opportunity that has never existed on the planet before: to come into a new world, an unimaginable new reality on this planet Earth; *or* we can come into an unimaginable disaster. The outcome depends on whether humans can go beyond their own personal horizon, transcend the limitations of their consciousness and embrace the new and larger possibilities of the Coming Avatāra.

Meditation on the Planetary Avatāra in the Heart

It is important that we prepare ourselves for, and become receptive to, the Coming Avatāra. There are two meditations that will help us achieve this. Firstly, if you are sensitive enough, you can try to feel within you the new, emerging energy of the Coming Avatāra.

This is difficult to do because, as mentioned previously, it is impossible for the New Avatāra to fully manifest all at once because it would cause too much of a disturbance on the planet. If the Avatāra were to release its consciousness into the planet all at once, if it focused its Cosmic Mind of Light onto the planet in its totality, the Earth would actually burn up. It would be like putting ten thousand volts of electricity through an ordinary light bulb. So the Planetary Avatāra works slowly, according to how we can respond to it.

The other meditation, which is much easier to do, is to tune into one of the past Avatāras to which you may have already been tuning in or already have some connection with because of Karma or cultural ties. Each of the past Avatāras had their own particular energy-field, so if you choose to meditate on, say, the Christ, Buddha, Lao Tzu or Our Lady[3] because you are subconsciously in tune with their energy-

---

[3] Our Lady, the Virgin Mary, was actually an Avatāra but not recognized as such by the church. She was known as Isis in Egypt and Quan Yin in China, two of Her major incarnations before She was the mother of Jesus. She was actually a greater Avatāra than Jesus, except that She played a supporting role for Him because the Hierarchy knew that the Jewish authorities were extremely materialistic and that it would not be an easy incarnation for Jesus because of all the opposition He would encounter. Before they sent down the Christ, therefore, the Hierarchy sent down Mary as a support for Jesus, who relied on Mary all the time (as well as the other Mary, Mary Magdalene, who also had a supporting role).

field, then the energy of that Avatāra will be activated inside you—the Love of the Christ, the Wisdom of the Buddha, the Motherliness of our Lady, and so on.

If you can learn this meditation technique and tune into one of the ancient Avatāras and feel their specific energy and work with it, then you will find that through that established energy-field you will connect with the vast energy-field of the New Avatāra. That's because the energies of the past Avatāras already exist in the planetary structure and all of those past energies will merge into the energy of the New Avatāra. This is the Divine Plan. The New Avatāra is all-embracing and completely enfolds, in its orbit of Infinite Intelligence, the entire planetary history from the beginning of time until now.

It is difficult to register the vibration of the New Energy because it is so vast, but you *can* identify with the tremendous, throbbing energy-field of Love of the Christ or the Wisdom energy-field of the Buddha or the caring, nurturing vibration of Our Lady. And through the old energy of that great being who changed the planet in their time, you can find the way into the Heart of the New Avatāra.

The technique for either meditation is quite simple: sit in a comfortable position, still your body, emotions and mind, focus your attention in the Heart area and try to sense either the New Avatāric Vibration or the energy-field of the past Avatāra of your choice.

About This Technique

The ultimate objective of this meditation is to tune into the energy of the past Avatāras who, because they are being absorbed into the future Avatāra, are actually no longer of the past but part of the future. The future Avatāra sweeps in with a tremendous all-encompassing energy. The Bible mentions "the seven Spirits who stand in front of the throne of the Deity" (REVELATION 4: 5). This refers to the great Cosmic Avatāras who worship the Deity in seven great radiant forms of Light—all of which are absorbed into the Coming Avatāra. So if you can tune into the energy of one of the past Avatāras and keep meditating on it and systematically working with it, it will reveal to you the future, quite literally.

*****

The important thing is to meditate in the Heart because that is the quickest way to the Kingdom of God. The whole idea is that your meditation has to be worshipful, like going to church in your Heart. You can go to a building—a mosque, synagogue or a church—to worship God, but in this meditation you worship God within your Heart, which is vastly different. Because God already exists in your Heart, you don't have to go to another building.

*****

The Gate of the Heart is opened through silence, prayer, visualizing your chosen God-form (in this case, one of the past Avatāras) or repeating a mantra of a God-form or a Divine Name, but whichever technique you use it has to be done with pure devotion, self-surrender, humility and simplicity. In the case of prayer, this "humility and simplicity" is very important. For example, "Our Father who art in Heaven, hallowed be thy Name" (MATTHEW 6: 9). It is simple and full of humility. Your ego, your personality, is not involved. You are not asking for something for yourself; rather, you are directing your attention to the Deity, glorifying the Deity for its own sake. So when you pray, pray like that, with surrender, humility and simplicity, because if your prayer gets complicated and your mind is too involved, you won't get anywhere.

By *prayer* we mean a longing to *become* divine, so whatever you say in your prayer should be oriented towards the Divine. You may choose a prayer which you invent yourself; it can be natural and spontaneous, just talking to the Deity Within in your own language and your own way, through your own mind. But the prayer has to be linked to the Deity, not asking for a new car or other material object. That won't bring you close to the Deity at all.

Then, when you connect to that past Avatāra and that prayer, silence, God-form, mantra or Divine Name becomes active in your Heart, you will feel first a warmth in your heart and later heat, like your whole body is full of fire, and then the heat becomes first Light and finally the Absolute Brilliant Light. When you reach the Light stage, you are already in the Buddhic dimension, the World of Unity, and when you reach the Brilliant Light, you are in the world of Nirvāṇa, the Kingdom of God, the Original Kingdom from which everything started. In other words, your chosen deity will ultimately take you to NIRVĀṆA, or to Liberation (MOKṢA), freedom from the Lower Worlds.

*****

The Hindu Scriptures talk about what Kṛṣṇa mainly did when He was a child because Kṛṣṇa is really the symbol of a child Avatāra—Love in its most innocent and purest form (whereas the Christ Love is strong, masculine, overwhelming in power and compassion). That's why the image of Kṛṣṇa is much loved by the Hindus: it represents innocence, how a child would love without any ego, ambition or self-ishness. Kṛṣṇa was an incarnation of the same entity who later became Jesus Christ, so you could say the Christ Love is a further development of the Kṛṣṇa Love.

*****

We have been working with the new energy-field for the last 30 years. If we had worked with an old energy-field, we would have had one mantra and a few rituals passed down by tradition, say, the Hindu, Jewish or Christian tradition, and we would have repeated the same spiritual formula all the time. But the energy we work with is the new Avatāric Energy, which is not fixed—which *can't* be fixed because it has to bring in the New. It's like looking for a new path through a forest. You still have to have the past as a basis—it's still the same old forest—otherwise the people coming behind you would not be able to relate to or approach the path at all. The old is there, but at the same time the new energy of the Avatāra is always seeking a new twist, a new turn, a new way through the old forest.

THE NINE PATHS TO ENLIGHTENMENT

It is important to understand that the New Planetary Avatāra cannot do everything on its own, in the same way that the CEO of a large company cannot do everything on his own. They both need workers. The Avatāra knows the Divine Plan for Humanity, but Humanity must respond and consciously help. In our natural state, however, we cannot receive the New Avatāric Energy without any preparation; it is too fine, of too high a vibration. We must therefore *do* something to refine ourselves and raise our natural vibration.

There are Nine Paths, or Gates, or Ways, to Enlightenment that a human being can follow at the moment. They are ancient and time-less and many thousands have gone through those Gates, walked down those Paths. You too must follow one of them, or some of them, *to prepare yourself* not only for the New Energy but also for the Glory that "the eye has not seen, nor ear has heard, nor has it been thought in the heart of man, what the Father prepared for them that Love Him" (1 CORINTHIANS 2: 9). These are the words of Jesus, but they are as applicable today as they were in the past and will be so in the future.

THE SEARCH
FOR EVERLASTING LIFE

We will begin with a general understanding of what Everlasting Life is, not just as facts about how things are but what you can do with those facts, because otherwise you will not understand why we have the Nine Paths to Enlightenment, or the Nine Gates to Everlasting Life.

When human beings were put on this planet a few million years ago, we descended from the higher regions of Creation, the Immortal Worlds. Technically, these are called NIRVĀṆA and the worlds above that, the worlds of Absolute Light, where Eternal Life is the norm—not something that you want or need to seek, but simply how you are by nature. Unfortunately, we have lost touch with those imperishable and indestructible realms and we have lost touch with our essential nature.

Since that time, from the very beginning of our creation, the human heart has always been searching for Immortality because within every one of us there is a sensation that there is something else we should be doing, or somewhere else we should be—another place, another condition, another realm of existence or another state of mind, heart or soul. So it is the fundamental nature of every human being, and of Humanity itself, to search for Immortality. It is the feeling that no matter what you have, it is never enough; no matter what you achieve, it is never enough; no matter how famous you become, it is never enough. The human heart is always unsatisfied. No matter how far we advance in technology, science, knowledge, power, personal attainment, it is never enough and it never will be enough.

Every single human being *is* a Living Soul and that Living Soul *has* a personality. Now that personality is "you" reading this paragraph at the moment. So "you" are two beings: you are a wonderful Living Soul, full of Light, blazing with glory, intelligence and understanding; and a personality enclosed in limited bodies in space and time. You as the Living Soul are always beautiful, always glorious, always wonderful, always in a state of harmony and love, and you as this personality are always having problems from the time you are born to the time you die, including the endless problems you have with other personalities.

As you can see, within your reality there is a big discrepancy or duality. There is the personality, which is changeable and always will be changeable; and there is the individual reality, your Soul, the real you, which is unchangeable, indestructible and eternal. So you as a Soul cannot die or be born and nothing can change you, *by your very nature*, because you are made of imperishable Light. On the other hand, your personality is a temporary manifestation. It's as if your eternal Soul decided to go on a temporary holiday—to this planet of all places!—and you are lucky if you reach the age of 100. But what is 100 years to the life of the immortal Soul? Nothing.

You need to understand this to see why you have been going wrong—why everybody has been going wrong—for millions of years. What people have always been doing, and what they are still doing, is focusing on the personality, trying to make *that* existence immortal. They believe that the physical body will live forever, that in this physical world you can create a heaven world for yourself and for Mankind, a glorious society where everybody will be blissed out. Forget it. Thinking that we can create a perfect life and society in this world, in this limited condition of space and time, with limited forms of energy, matter and embodiment is a major fault in human thinking, because this particular condition is not meant for that.

The reason is that the same duality existing inside you exists also in the Cosmos. There is a bright Reality that is eternal, always stable, perfect and ideal, and there is *this* reality, this world that is always restless and is not (and never can be) perfect and ideal. You can of course try to improve it, but it will never reach the level of perfection of the Soul on the spiritual dimensions.

The restless world includes the physical dimensions, the astral dimensions (the after-death world) and the mental dimensions, what we call the Three Worlds, the temporary "passing-away worlds". All the humans locked up in those dimensions are under the delusion that somehow they can make their world eternal and perfect. People in the Physical World believe that achieving success in life is what life is all about and even people in the Heaven World (the Mental World) have the delusion that Heaven lasts forever and there is nothing beyond the joys and happiness of that world.

It is important to understand this because then you will understand the idea of seeking for Enlightenment, or Everlasting Life: where it comes from, why it is and how to actually achieve it in this lifetime.

So there is a general delusion, or Māyā, in the Three Worlds and the human species is caught up in it. This means that, basically, you have been operating on wrong knowledge all your life, so you have to give up certain wrong ideas. The first of these is that you are perfect. You have to give up this idea immediately otherwise you will never manifest the True, the truly perfect *inside* you. Next you have to give up the idea that other people are perfect and you therefore expect that they will always do the right thing, say the right thing and behave in the right way. You also have to give up the idea that your society is perfect, that the particular political system you live under is perfect.

In other words, you need to reconsider the way you look at everything, and once you understand the imperfection, the changeability, the impossibility of the situation, you won't expect politicians to be what they are not, you won't expect religious leaders to be what they are not, you won't expect anybody to be what they are not. Then you will understand why society is always struggling, why people are always fighting, why politicians and religions are always fighting (and why we always have Spiritual Teachers trying to improve the chaotic conditions of human society). Then you will understand the impermanence of *this* nature and what is really the Permanent, the True and the Beautiful. And then you are free.

The real permanency is *within* the impermanent; the eternal, shining Light within you is inside that which is perishable and changeable. It is *that* which you have to discover, and when you do the way you look at life radically changes. You will work with the everlasting principle of the Light within you, to bring that principle to everybody in this world. So you are not trying to change the outer conditions, but trying to bring the Inner Condition into this world. It is a completely different approach to life. You become a Spiritual Teacher, a Wise Person, you show people their frailty and imperfection but you tell them that within them there is the real thing—the undying, eternal, imperishable, ever-loving and ever-perfect Reality that everybody must find.

Only when this has been found by everybody can there be major improvements in society and glorious changes on this planet. The intention of people trying to improve this life is good, but their approach is wrong. They are doing it with an empty bucket.

If you have a bucket with a hole in it and use it to get water for your garden, then by the time you get back to the garden the water has run out of the bucket and you can't water the garden. In other words, our approach in this physical life has been wrong from the beginning because we have discarded that which is real and true: the Immortal, the Imperishable, the Divine. Once you discard that then everything you do cannot be right because it is not based on the fundamental truth or the fundamental reality of Nature, because behind all Nature, behind every human being, is the Divine Essence, the Perfection, the Ideal, the Beauty, the Truth. You have to find that *first*—rather than continually reshuffling political ideas, psychological ideas, philosophical ideas or social ideas—before you can make any real changes.

This understanding can bring about a fundamental change in your view of life, a complete reversal in the way you think about yourself, about others, about human society and about all the changes happening around planetary transformation. It is the teaching of the Masters and the great Sages who have *attained*, who have completed the goal of human destiny and human evolution and have worked out the meaning of life—and lived it. In their view, you accept things as they are, that people are imperfect, that conditions are imperfect, that no matter what you do on this planet it will be imperfect. Then, knowing that *within* that is the perfection, you live in the two realities simultaneously.

In the chapter on the First Gate, we explain that the average human being is continually fighting against their own nature, the nature of others, the nature of society and the nature of Nature itself, so naturally they do not know that they should switch their attention to the Inner Reality, that which is truly permanent and real. The more you tune into your immortal Soul, the more you understand what your personality is about and whether it is helping or hindering the evolution of the planet. You may think you are doing good, trying to help people, but you may not necessarily be doing good. It is only when you are established in the Soul that you really know what is good. Being in the Light of Reality as it shines in the here and now is what is good, and only from that can the right outer transformation come. If you are in the Light, if you understand the Light within you, you live in a completely different reality; you are then a Sage, a Master, a Teacher.

A Teacher doesn't have to be an educated person or have a university degree or be famous. The Inner Teacher is in the Soul of that being, not in the outer peculiarities. Every Teacher has peculiarities, that is, a personality, which they need to be able to function in this physical dimension. But there are many Masters who don't retain their personality because they don't teach others. They attain Enlightenment and absorb themselves into a transcendental condition, which is fine for them but doesn't help the guy next door. Those who are truly compassionate—we call them the Masters of Wisdom and Compassion—retain their old personalities that they had before Enlightenment and through that personality they work to help Humanity.

So the personality is important, but remember: the personality is not *the* important thing. It is simply the instrument through which you connect to this world, where you need to function, an instrument through which you can work for others.

You are lucky to be getting this knowledge. Many people live in places where the physical circumstances are such that there is no chance to have this knowledge, there are no Teachers of the Esoteric Wisdom, no books on the subject. And many have the chance but are not interested because they do not have that something inside that resonates to the Truth Principle, they do not seek Immortality or they look for it in physical life, in outer things. They try to make their job perfect, to earn more money, they try to attain more position and power, because they think that somehow their satisfaction in life will come through outer physical activities and things. But the more you seek fame and glory in this world, the farther you go from Immortality.

It is important to understand how the *Search for Everlasting Life* is happening today in the New Age. Major changes are happening on this planet now; things are no longer done as they were in the previous Piscean Age. The planet is in a crisis condition and that crisis is much more than just the normal changes that occur when going from one age to another. We are having a *crisis of understanding*, of understanding who we are as human beings on this planet, and this crisis stretches across the entire globe.

Every human being is a field of energy and we are all interlinked—every human being influences every other human being—so when billions of people are living in the wrong way, sending out a wrong energy vibration, it has a destructive effect on the whole planet. Energy is always in motion; it has to manifest itself. These wrong energies have been building up for thousands of years and Mother Earth is now at the point where She has to release the tension with a massive, primal scream, in the same way that human beings release built-up anger and frustration. So Mother Earth has to react to the situation. And how does She release these energies? By unleashing tornadoes, hurricanes, earthquakes, floods and fires. (And it is going to get worse because there is still a great deal of pent-up energy that has to be released.) This has nothing to do with philosophy or religion. It has to do with energy; every energy has a result.

In the Bhagavad-Gītā, Kṛṣṇa said, "At every age when there is chaos, lawlessness and disharmony, I come again and again." "At every age" is not referring to an astrological age. He is not saying that he is coming at the end of the Piscean Age or the beginning of the Aquarian Age. He is referring to an age when the density of the planet is so heavy and the disharmony of Humanity is so great that a cosmic interference *has* to happen to rectify the situation, to bring it back in line with the original Plan. There is a plan for the evolution of the planet in the Divine Mind. When we are continually destroying that plan, the Divine Mind sends down some help. And this is what is happening now with the Coming Avatāra.

As mentioned in the preceding chapter, in previous times a tremendous Energy came from the inner dimensions, from the Worlds of Light, through a single personality who tried to reconfigure human consciousness in that particular society, whether it was in India, the Middle East or China, in the hope that from that society the new energy-wave would spread out to the larger planetary society. But the Coming Avatāra is a multidimensional reality. This means the Avatāra will come through many Masters, many Teachers and many ways that have never happened before, and this is because of the real crisis on the planet, a crisis the planet has never experienced before. Now the Avatāra is coming in a subtle way and impacting anybody who is able to receive it.

The Coming Avatāra is a *cosmic* Avatāra, but no matter how grand and glorious it is, it has to work through people—people who are able to do its work. If there is nobody able to do that, the Avatāra will just remain in its own high-frequency vibration; that's all it can do. So the Avatāra can only work through you. You have to understand that your very person and life are a channel through which you can help the

Avatāra manifest the glory of the Divine Plan. If you don't do it, who else will? There will always be a few people who respond, and they are responding at present, but it is not enough that only a few people rise to the challenge. It is meaningless because it is now a planetary problem; practically every country on the planet is dysfunctional in one way or another. The task is enormous, almost superhuman, but we will have the help of the Avatāra if we do the right thing ourselves.

In the olden days, Noah was told to build a boat because a big flood was coming. Of course everybody just laughed because Israel was a desert in those days and he was miles away from the sea. Well, he did build a boat, and the rains came. He was the only person who was responsive *within himself.* We have a similar situation now. We have to build a boat of Salvation for all of Humanity, the seven billion people incarnated on this planet and the rest who are in the Inner Worlds, so that they can penetrate the inner dimensions, the permanent and eternal Spiritual Reality within themselves and within the planet. Then, the big transformation can happen.

In my book *Planetary Transformation*[4] I mentioned that Humanity has been given the grace of up to about 300 years to transform itself. If it fails, we will return to the old ways of war and disharmony, with the normal suffering and diseases. So we have some time to look at this situation, how we caused it and what we as Humanity can do about it. And this is where this teaching comes in. For the last thirty years we have being teaching the idea of spiritual regeneration through the Way of Wisdom and the Way of Love, the importance of working along those lines, because if we transform ourselves individually we

[4] Imre Vallyon, *Planetary Transformation: A Personal Guide to Embracing Planetary Change* (Sounding-Light Publishing, 2010).

transform the world. Energy cannot be stopped or contained within walls, so our function is to generate the New Energy that will enable the planet to go through this tremendous cosmic transformation—safely, sanely and perfectly.

THE WAY OF THE SPIRITUAL WARRIOR

Cultivation

The First Gate is the *Way of the Spiritual Warrior*. To introduce this to you I will tell you about how we started our Spiritual School in New Zealand, because it's exactly what the Way of the Spiritual Warrior is about. When we bought the place there was only grass and countryside and farmland, with wild pigs, goats and sheep running around everywhere. So the first thing we did was put a fence around the property to keep out the wild animals. Then, over the years, we planted trees and plants and created gardens.

The spiritual lesson of this is what we call *cultivation*, which is what the Way of the Warrior is about. When you start the Spiritual Path you are like our School used to be: wild and uncultivated, with just your natural personality. So long as you let your personality remain as it is, there's no progress for you in this life in terms of the true meaning of existence, which is the attainment of Enlightenment, or Eternal Life. And this is where hundreds of millions of people fail. They stay as they are, without thinking, "This is not really all there is to it. I should be doing something else or be more than what I am."

So the first thing in Spiritual Life is to decide that you should do something about your basic nature, that you should become cultivated on the personality level.

To FOLLOW THE FIRST GATE, YOU HAVE TO CULTIVATE HARMLESSNESS, NON-AGGRESSIVENESS, PEACEFULNESS, TRANQUILLITY AND LOVINGNESS.[5]

You have to cultivate these five qualities, or virtues, because they are the basis of the Way of the Spiritual Warrior, and because they are precisely the qualities that are lacking in society. Society has many police and military people, many aggressive, violent people. Basically, the human being is harmful and aggressive, does not make peace, does not like tranquillity and has no love. That has been the basic nature of the human family for the last few hundred thousand years. So the violent qualities human beings exhibit in society have to be neutralized by cultivating harmlessness, non-aggressiveness, peacefulness, tranquillity and lovingness.

You have to practise cultivating these qualities twenty-four hours a day, and it's not as easy as it may sound. If an insect bites you, you have to be peaceful and loving to the little bug. What is more, you have to develop these qualities on every level—you have to be *physically* harmless, *emotionally* harmless and *mentally* harmless. There is not much point to being harmless on the physical level if your mind is full of evil thoughts about other people. This is why the people who are into the warrior arts but haven't got these qualities will never make it to the true state of Enlightenment.

---

[5] This statement and other statements set apart from the normal text throughout this book are statements of truths perceived in Cosmic Consciousness and then expressed as short aphorisms that the mind can hold onto and work with.

Of course, you will fail over and over again, but that's fine; you are not expected to acquire these virtues right away. The goal is to watch yourself, and when you see that you are getting angry for whatever reason, go back to the cultivation of tranquillity and peacefulness. The fact that you notice what has happened and try to re-establish yourself in these virtues means you are already on the way.

Over the millennia, many false teachings have come into spirituality—because people always expect somebody else to do the work for them. For example, the Christians believe that they will be saved because Jesus Christ suffered for their sins. What a foolish idea! Jesus Christ was crucified 2,000 years ago and He certainly did a lot of good for His followers, but to believe that forever afterwards He is going to suffer for you (no matter how foolish you are) is really an enormous ignorance. No, the Guru can help you, the Spiritual Hierarchy can help you, but you must cultivate yourself. That's a primary requisite.

If you want to follow the Way of the Spiritual Warrior, you have to become harmless, non-aggressive and peaceful, do everything with a tranquil mind and be full of love for all your neighbours. Otherwise you will not even make it *to* the First Gate.

The Simple Way

The Way of the Spiritual Warrior has an active side and a passive side, and most people in the martial arts field only know about the active side—doing judo or karate or kung fu, using drive and force. Very few of them know about the passive side, which is the true mark of the Spiritual Warrior. One way you can understand the passive side is through what the Ancients called the *Simple Way*.

The Simple Way means that you reduce your excess baggage. By *excess baggage* we mean your education, your family structure, your social customs, your culture, your race—whatever conditions you. Everybody carries a huge burden: I'm a Hindu, I'm a Buddhist, I'm a Maori, I'm a Jew; all the stress, traumas and blame related to what everybody said and did to you since the time you were born; all the stuff you learned in school that you will never use in your life. It is all excess baggage and it all has to go, because it's not the real You, the real Self.

To become a Master Warrior you have to discover the Simple Way. What are you now, without all your conditioning? What you are now is the reality. You get rid of everything of the past and become simple: *just you, now.*

Just So

Just So is a good expression meaning "just who you are and what you are in the here and now", without all your thinking about what you were in the past and will be in the future, without all the baggage you carry inside.

The Master Warriors of the past were always in the *Just So* condition, and they were invincible. If they were in a real sword fight and suddenly remembered something uncle Joe had said to them years ago, they would have lost their concentration—and their head. They had to be in the state of *Just So*, free from excess baggage with their total attention in that very moment, in that very action. Otherwise, their life would have been finished.

Nowadays we don't have to fight with swords, but the Way of the Warrior, the way to attain Everlasting Life, is still the same: We have to be full of the virtues of harmlessness, non-aggressiveness, peacefulness, tranquillity and lovingness. And we have to live in the *Just So* condition. That's why this Path is the easiest and at the same time the hardest. To be *Just So* is easy and difficult.

Warrior Meditation: Surrendering the Ego to the Heart

This is a meditation that will speed up the attainment of being in the here and now so that you can express the *Just So* condition directly and spontaneously. The technique is called *Surrendering the Ego to the Heart*, and with practice, the *Just So* condition will become your natural state of being.

First, however, you have to understand the ego and the Heart. The ego is you, the personality with all the baggage you have been carrying with you all your life. The Heart, or the Spiritual Heart, is a beautiful translucent Light inside you, beyond the dimensions of space and time, pulsating with Love, Bliss and Joy. *Surrender the ego* means you surrender all your thoughts and emotions, your past and future, and you surrender by letting them go and switching your attention from the ego to the Heart.

This is the difficult part of it because your ego wants to think, it wants to feel, it is restless and wants to do something. You have to surrender everything that you are and be in the *Just So* condition, without the desire to become a Spiritual Warrior, without the desire to become anything. Then, in that state of *just being*, you switch your attention from your ego to the Heart, the immortal Self within you. In that act of surrender you merge into the Heart and the First Gate to Immortal Life opens by itself; you don't have to do anything.

If you *try* to be in the Heart, if you try to enter the Heart through aggressiveness, desire or force, you will never make it. That is why it is important that you practise the virtues of harmlessness, non-aggressiveness, peacefulness, tranquillity and lovingness in your normal living conditions so that they become second nature. When the Gate opens, you expand towards the Cosmos and the Cosmos implodes inside you and you become an infinite Cosmic Being—all-knowing, all-understanding, all-compassionate and all-wise. Wisdom and Love are not learned from a book. You already are Wisdom; you already are Love.

Surrendering the Ego to the Heart

Rest your awareness in the Spiritual Heart Centre. Remain quiet and still. Let go of all the thoughts, feelings and desires of the past, present and future and surrender your ego to the Heart. Switch your attention to the Heart itself, that true, shining Soul-Reality within you. Just be!

About This Technique

This meditation is also called *Being in the Stillness of the Tao in the Heart*. Tao, which is the Chinese word for the Sanskrit word PARABRAHMAN, the Supreme Reality, has two parts: Stillness, which is on the transcendental level, and Activity, which is the dynamic part that acts through all of Nature, meaning all the *created* worlds—the Physical, Astral and Mental Worlds. Similarly, in Christianity there is the Father, Son and Holy Spirit. The "Father" is the transcendental region, the Unmanifest; the "Son" represents the Light Worlds; and the "Holy Spirit" is the part of the Deity that is active in Creation. In the Kabbalah, *Yahweh* is the Father aspect, the inactive part of Reality, and *Shekinah* is the active part.

In this meditation, therefore, you sit still and try to sense that part of Tao, or the Ultimate Reality, which is immobile, motionless, absolutely stable and steady. Once you sense that All-Embracing Oneness, you will enter the Heart, the Gate to the higher dimensions, the spiritual realities.

*****

The active part of Creation is always active, from the beginning of Creation to the end, and the still part of Creation is always still. This is represented by the Chinese Yin-Yang symbol, which shows the Oneness and the eternal motion of Duality.

*****

When you experience complete identification with the Heart, you remain in stillness, that is, you observe the activity of Creation without involving yourself in it; you sense the interplay between the various polarities in Creation but it doesn't disturb the stillness. It's very much like the Zen example of sitting on the riverbank and watching the river flowing by. You are sitting still and are simply aware of the coming and going of energies, the coming and going of thoughts, phenomena, experiences, the appearing and disappearing of the ego—all in that continuum of silence, stillness and oneness, all in a warm sense of loving Unity.

*****

Practise this Spiritual Warrior meditation in order to stabilize yourself in the Heart and always remain in that state, even when you are not meditating. Meditation is a fixed practice but ultimately you have to have a sense of unity, stillness and peace at the same time that you are busily active in the world; you have to be active physically, emotionally and mentally without losing that sensation of total stillness. That is when you become a Master Warrior.

The Spiritual Warrior and the Heart

THE LIFE OF THE SPIRITUAL WARRIOR IS HEART-FOCUSED.
THE HEART CONNECTS TO ALL THINGS.

The Spiritual Warrior surrenders the ego to the Heart and works from the impulse that comes from the Heart. This means the whole *life* of the Spiritual Warrior is Heart-focused, and because the Heart connects to all things it becomes the Warrior's sensory mechanism.

Normal warriors trained in the martial arts use the Solar Plexus Centre, which is a far more primitive sensory mechanism than the Heart. They awaken their Solar Plexus Centre through breathing techniques that open up the Astral World, so they can sense visible and invisible objects around them and know where danger is coming from. But Heart awareness is on a much higher level than solar plexus awareness because it works through the Light-energy within the Heart that emanates from the Spiritual Heart. Spiritual Warriors can sense all things because they are connected to all things through the Heart. So they know whether a situation is right or wrong, whether a person is right or wrong, whether an enemy is a real enemy or a friend is a real friend. Spiritual Warriors cannot be deceived because the Heart cannot be deceived.

The important point is that you can understand the Way of the Spiritual Warrior only to the degree that you can actually live *from* the Heart and *in* the Heart. It is not a thought process. There are too many people in the world who are focused in the mind. They go where the Opposition moves them, just like chess pieces, and they will never be Spiritual Warriors. But you cannot fight with just thoughts; you need the real Light-energy, the inner Light within you that thoughts cannot touch. That is why your life has to revolve around the Spiritual

Awareness inside you and why you have to be Heart-centred right from the beginning, if you want to become a Spiritual Warrior.

WHERE THERE IS DARKNESS, THE HEART SHOWS THE WAY.

Where there is darkness means that where there is indecision or conflicting opinions about a person or situation or about yourself or your goal in life, there is darkness; that is, you are unable to act because you cannot see the way. *The Heart shows the way* means that the Heart is infallible. The Heart is connected to Buddhi, a subtle Light-energy that is a combination of Wisdom (profound understanding) and Love (total compassion). Once that Light-energy is activated in the Heart, it can show you exactly the right way, the right solution.

Normally, when you are in darkness your mind becomes very busy. You can ask a hundred people and receive a hundred different answers and your mind will agonize over the answers—while the darkness remains. But rather than analysing the situation in your mind, simply forget the whole thing and put your attention in the Heart. Allow your mind to become silent and, if you have already learned to feel that subtle energy inside you, the Heart will tell you what course of action to take, not in spoken words or ideas but as a *knowing*, an inner impulse that tells you which way to go.

In the beginning of this process many people, after descending into the Heart and feeling the right solution, still do exactly what the mind wants because they think the mind is cleverer! Of course, they get the wrong answer and are back where they started, in darkness. It takes courage to obey the impulses of the Heart, especially when the Heart gives you an answer that the mind fights against.

There is an interesting and profound scene in the Chinese warrior movie *House of Flying Daggers* where the hero and heroine warriors decide for some reason to separate from each other. The hero leaps on his horse and, with hair flowing in the wind, gallops far into the forest. And then he stops. He remains still for a long time, sitting on his horse, while the leaves fall all about him. He is searching his Heart. The decision he previously made was from the mind; he thought that leaving was the best action to take. But being a Spiritual Warrior, he pauses, enters the Heart and without any words he knows the right thing to do: he turns his horse around and goes back in the direction he came.

So part of the lesson of the Spiritual Warrior is to trust your Heart without interference from the mind. This requires preliminary practice whereby you develop the ability to drop your consciousness into the Heart and learn to feel that you are alive in the Heart. You already live in the Heart! Not your physical heart, of course, but the inner regions of the Spiritual Heart, where you quite literally dwell as a Living Soul; where Ātman, the Spirit, the Self within you, resides. Once you enter the Heart, be still and feel the Heart, and trust whatever comes from that Life-essence inside you.

HARMONY IS MAINTAINED BY BEING CENTRED IN THE HEART.

Generally speaking, women are luckier because they are more connected to the Heart than men. Nowadays, of course, because of the education system, girls become as intellectual as boys and never even know that the Heart exists, and nobody learns how to feel from the Heart or how to live from the Heart. It's what I call the disaster of education—a disaster from the spiritual point of view because it keeps people focused on the material objectives of a material world, as if nothing else existed. If learning about this world were only a part of their education, that would be fine, but there is no mention of the other worlds, the other realities; no one is taught that they are part of a *larger* structure. So human beings are kept nicely in the material plane, living materialistically, wasting their wonderful human life.

Everything in this society is done through the mind: you fight for this cause or that cause, for this opinion or that opinion, and the other person does exactly the same, so there is endless fighting and disharmony. There is no aspect of human life that is in harmony. Why? Because ideas and opinions conflict with each other and there is no Understanding. If you are a Warrior who lives in the Heart, your inner being is always in a state of harmony, equilibrium and balance. The Spiritual Heart does not experience conflict. The radiation of the Heart is always in harmony because the Buddhic energy of Love-Wisdom is a harmonious energy—it cannot be anything else. It is not possible to imagine a *loving* energy or an energy full of *wisdom* that is not in a state of harmony.

When you are Heart-centred, you can remain harmonious in your day-to-day life in all your relationships with people at home and at work. If the other person is working through the mind, you can make a suggestion from the Heart. If the person accepts it, that's fine; if the person doesn't accept it, that's also fine. Why? Because the integrity of the Heart says that you cannot force your ideas on other people. The Light has to work in a person by agreement of that person. It is up to the other person to feel your Heart-energy and the sincerity behind your suggestion. When you explain things from the Heart, even mind-oriented people can feel the positive energy emanating from you, and even though their mind may not understand the suggestion, they will likely follow your advice.

IDENTIFICATION WITH THE SPIRIT WITHIN THE HEART IS THE CENTRE OF STABILITY.

We have talked about the action of the Heart when you are able to sense the energy of the Heart, how it acts in the Way of Wisdom and the Way of Love. But now we go one stage deeper into the mystery: Identification with the Spirit within the Heart is the centre of stability. Here you do not just feel the loving, all-wise energy coming out of the Heart and act from there, but you go deeper to *identifying* with it. This is what the Indian Yogīs call *Yoga*, what the Christian, Jewish and Muslim Mystics call *Union*, that is, 'at-one-ness' with the Spirit within the Heart. That energy emanates from Ātman, the Higher Self, or the point of Divinity above the Buddhic dimension. It is our Spiritual Being and is also called the God-Self or the God Within.

You reach this stage of identification as a result of two things: (1) regular meditation using techniques such as *Surrendering the Ego to the Heart* and rhythmic intonation of the *Warrior Mantra*[6]; and (2) actually *living* the life of the Heart. Meditation alone will not take you through any one of the Gates; your whole *life* has to change. Many people following various religious or spiritual paths meditate every day and still get nowhere because their whole life, their inner consciousness, their inner *reality* has not transformed. In the Way of the Warrior, you have to have spiritual practices *and* a fundamentally transformed life. Then, at a certain point, there comes the stage of *identification* with the Spirit within.

Once you reach that stage, you will look at things from the inside out. Before, you were looking at everything from the outside and taking it in. You may have had a decision to make or a disagreement with someone,

---

[6] See the Warrior Mantra practice at the end of this chapter.

so you brought the matter back into the Heart; you were working from the outside in. But now you are looking at all situations and problems in life in a reverse way. That's why it's difficult for the average person to understand the actions of a person who is identified with the Spirit within, a person who is looking at things from inside out.

When you are centred within the Heart and identified with the Spirit within, you are looking at the overall flow of the Vital Force as it moves outward into Creation from within. You are with that force and therefore see where it comes from and how it's going to work out, *instantaneously*, because you are right at the centre of stability. The Spirit within is always stable, like a solid wall of immovable Light, so you are in that stability all the time and therefore your attitude to life is different, the way you do things is different and your understanding is different, including your understanding of the Warrior Path itself.

The Spiritual Warrior and Nature

To attain Enlightenment, or Immortality, it is a primary necessity to be in tune with Nature. Nature is a direct link between us and the Absolute, the Ultimate Reality, so if we are out of tune with Nature we have no chance to experience the Absolute. This is expressed by the following fundamental Warrior principle:

THE WAY OF THE SPIRITUAL WARRIOR IS TO FLOW WITH NATURE, WHICH IS THE GATEWAY TO THE ABSOLUTE.

Humanity is massively out of tune with Nature. People are becoming more enslaved to mechanical gadgets, computers and virtual reality and less aware of even what is happening inside their own bodies. When somebody is meant to die by Destiny or Karma, they are put on life-support machines or their life is prolonged a few more months or years by transplanting body parts from other people. This has become common now and it is completely wrong by nature. If you are meant to die, you should die; otherwise, you are fighting against Nature, and that has karmic results. Nature works according to certain laws in the perishable dimensions—the physical, astral and mental dimensions—and we have to obey the laws of Nature in order to obtain Enlightenment.

Large numbers of human beings live nowhere near Nature, let alone are in tune with Nature. It's a crisis point for Humanity and it is important for you as an individual: if you cannot tune into Nature you cannot be a Spiritual Warrior. Period.

As a child you were more attuned to Nature. Small children can sense the life-force in the grass, the sky, the stars at night, a beautiful flower, a cat or a dog, and they get all excited about it. Then as they grow up and become educated and mentally orientated, they become out of tune with Nature (and with themselves and others). In olden times people were far more connected with Nature, more aware of plants, birds, animals, the weather and the seasons. That level of attunement has disappeared in so-called civilized modern man; we now live in concrete jungles and read about Nature in books or visit it when we go on holidays. Being in touch with Nature means that you are in touch with Nature all the time.

As a human being you are absolutely interconnected with Nature, and Nature expresses itself fully in *you* because you are the primary object of Nature; that is to say, the Human Being is Nature's great work of art.

As you become more aware of the natural world, you will notice that the cycle of birth, growth, decay and death is everywhere, that Nature is not all positive and constructive but also destructive. Understanding this will broaden your experience of reality because that duality—the positive and the negative, the good and the bad, the creative and the destructive—is inside you, just like in Nature. To reach the First Gate you need to understand this duality, understand why things are often contradictory and opposing each other, and then go beyond that into the Oneness, the state of Liberation and Freedom. But first you have to *see* Nature, without judgement.

I have a problem when I see a cat catching a mouse or a spider catching a fly. I always want to save the mouse or the fly! If you are compassionate towards one creature, you harm the other; in this case there would be no food for the cat or the spider. This situation occurs everywhere in Nature and will be a dilemma for you on the way to becoming a Spiritual Warrior because it will raise many questions of what is the right action to take.

The secret of the Spiritual Warrior is to accept things as they are, and you can do this by truly observing Nature and understanding how it is. The sunshine gives life and it can burn you; the rain gives life and takes it away with floods. You can condemn the sunshine and you can condemn the rain, or you can accept it all as part of Nature. If you accept it then you are free; if you condemn it you are bound and cannot attain the state of harmlessness, non-aggressiveness, peaceful-ness, tranquillity and lovingness. When you comprehend Nature in its totality and accept things as they are, then you will be able to accept yourself and express those virtues effortlessly.

What I am trying to say is that if you really have those qualities inside you, you will treat every human being, every animal and every species of life differently. The Way of the Spiritual Warrior is to flow with Nature, the gateway to the Absolute. So when you are in Nature, try to tune into and feel the energy of the ground, the sky, the trees, the plants, and be aware of how all that life is interconnected. Tune into as much of Nature as you can because that will help you transcend Nature and go to the Absolute. You have to go beyond Nature, and you cannot go beyond Nature until you tune into Nature.

ALL THINGS ARE INTERDEPENDENT.

Every human being is an energy-field. Every living species is an energy-field. And what is important is that all of these energy-fields are interrelated. We can use the symbol of the Cross to illustrate the interdependence of all things: the horizontal arm of the Cross represents the interdependence of all living things in this physical world, the interdependence of the Human Kingdom, the Animal Kingdom and the Plant Kingdom. The secret is, however, that there is also an interdependence between the Inner Worlds, represented by the vertical arm of the Cross. So the Physical World is dependent on the Astral World, which is dependent on the Causal World, which is dependent on the Buddhic World, which is dependent on the Nirvāṇic World, which is dependent on the worlds beyond Nirvana. In other words, the interdependence reaches throughout all of Nature on the Physical Plane and all the way up through the Inner Worlds to the Absolute.

Understanding this is the key to your Liberation and the key to liberating society, but it is also part of the difficulty of being human, because we all depend on one another. What is more, the interdependence is absolute: you cannot isolate yourself from impacting on other people or others impacting on you. As humans we also impact on the invisible energy-fields of animals and plants. For example, you can approach a beautiful primeval forest and feel an antagonism coming towards you because you are a human being. We are systematically destroying the forests so there is a subconscious part of the forest that understandably does not like us because we are so destructive. So it is possible to feel how Nature reacts to us; furthermore, we can change Nature by our right reaction to it.

There was a great Indian Saint who was one day walking up the hill to his ashram when he accidentally stood on a beehive. The bees rushed out and stung him many times. Everyone knew he was a Saint but the bees didn't know that! Just because he was a Saint it didn't mean that Nature would stop working in the way that it works. There is another story from India about a Guru who was meditating in the jungle. His disciples knew of a herd of elephants that was coming straight towards him, trampling everything in its path. They ran to him and tried to wake him out of his deep meditation, but he refused to move, saying that he was united with God and the elephants would not hurt him. His disciples still picked him up and moved him out of the way. If they hadn't used their common sense the Saint would have been trampled. In other words, he didn't understand the laws of Nature; he was not functioning *with* the laws of Nature.

Irrespective of how we view Nature, Nature has its own way and *we* have to tune into Nature, not the other way around. Only when we work *with* Nature can we be liberated. There is a tendency for human beings to superimpose their ideas on Nature, what they think it is or should be. A typical example is how people are frightened of spiders and feel that they are the most terrible of creatures. But that is just a projection of the mind; spiders are not like that at all. The Way of the Spiritual Warrior is the way of Nature: to observe reality as it is and not project ideas onto reality. Remove your ideas of who a person is; remove your ideas of the situation you are in. Only when you experience people and situations as they really are do you become truly harmless, truly non-aggressive, truly peaceful, truly tranquil and truly loving.

Sensing How Nature Works Within You

This is a Spiritual Warrior meditation technique for tuning into yourself: *Sensing How Nature Works Within You.*

First, centre your awareness in the Heart and then have the general sensation of harmlessness, tranquillity, peacefulness and lovingness, of just *being there*, in the state of quietude. Try to feel how Nature, the life-force that sustains your physical body, is working inside you. Then try to go beyond that to how your emotions are working inside you and then how your mind is working. Feel how you are in *this* moment, not how you were yesterday or will be tomorrow.

Simply experience what is there, without condemnation, criticism or judgement, without mental descriptions, and then as your experience goes deeper and deeper into your body, your emotions, your mind, suddenly drop everything. This is the part that is so difficult, because at that moment you do nothing. You move from activity into non-doing and become Pure Being, just awareness of yourself without a name, without a quality: you are no longer a good person or a bad person, young or old, American or Chinese. Suddenly there is nothing but You. Then you understand the Way of the Spiritual Warrior.

The Warrior of Light

At this particular time, in light of the major changes I described in my book *Planetary Transformation*, the First Gate, the Way of the Spiritual Warrior, is the most important gate in terms of what is happening on the planet. Our Mother Earth is presently undergoing a process of rebirth, trying to be reborn into a higher level of consciousness, and She is struggling. Rebirth means change—you have to be something other than what you were before—and there is always an opposition to that, forces that do not want change, that want things to stay exactly as they are. This process is setting in motion the great Warrior Path, the struggle between the Warriors of Light and the Warriors of Darkness, the constructive and destructive powers on the planet. This is why the Way of the Spiritual Warrior is so important for these troubled times.

There are many books written about 2012 and about the end of the world, and many of them talk about ecology, the atmosphere, the oceans and other environmental issues, without giving any spiritual context whatsoever. They all think that the big transformation will come about by changing the way we treat the environment on this *physical* dimension. But that is only on the surface of things; it is not the major change at all.

The big change is the fight between the Light and the Darkness, between the evolutionary forces and the destructive forces within the planet. If you have studied the Spiritual Sciences or the ancient scriptures, you are aware that this fight has been going on for hundreds of thousands of years. In the Indian scriptures, for example, there are stories about wars between gods, goddesses and demons, and the Bible talks about the "wars in Heaven" (REVELATION 12: 7) between angelic hierarchies. Of course the materialists do not want to know about wars in Heaven or Warriors of Light and Warriors of Darkness—they are all mythologies or fairy tales for them. But those events in the scriptures were real and, more importantly, they are taking place at this very moment and on a much larger scale. This is why we need Spiritual Warriors, Warriors of Light—Warriors who work with the Light, for the Light and by the Light.

In the olden days Warriors went forth on a spiritual quest for Enlightenment or Transformation, but now the entire planet is on a spiritual quest and this quest depends on us, every single human being. If we are successful, the planet will be transformed; if not, the chaos and darkness will continue in an even larger way. During the First and Second World Wars we allowed the planet to degenerate and come under the control of the negative forces of materialism, which blocked off the Light from human consciousness altogether. That was the same crisis situation that had occurred during the times of Lemuria and Atlantis, when the negative forces were so overwhelming that the Spiritual Hierarchy had to destroy those civilizations so that the planet would not become one of the Dark Planets.

Although it went against Cosmic Law, the Spiritual Hierarchy had to interfere during the World Wars and they released angelic hierarchies in the mental, astral and etheric-physical dimensions to neutralize the negative forces and help the positive forces win. The only problem is, those times were our last chances. According to the Law of Life, every human being (and every angel) has to have free will and not be coerced into doing anything they don't want to. Now the rule is going to be upheld. Now we have to purify our planet by ourselves. Now we have to be Warriors of Light and stand up against the Darkness, liberate the planet and be free, through our own understanding.

The urgency and importance of this is that over the next few decades the conflict between the Forces of Light and the Forces of Darkness will increase, day by day, month by month, year by year. The planetary repercussions will also increase as the inner structure of the planet is shaken up and Mother Earth convulses, producing more floods, tornadoes, earthquakes and hurricanes. You could say that our Mother Earth is having a nervous breakdown on a cosmic scale, because the negative forces are so strong they are swamping the positive Light-energies. So we have to help Mother Earth on the inner levels and work with the Light-energy to purify the etheric-physical and astral dimensions of the negative forces.

In *Planetary Transformation* I mentioned the need to make a choice: to be on the side of the Light or on the side of the Darkness. Remember what the Christ said: "He who is not with me is against me" (MATTHEW 12: 30). The Christ, the Buddha, Rama, Kṛṣṇa, Lao Tzu were all Warriors of Light in their day. Light is an evolutionary energy, an upward-moving energy or force, and those great beings brought in the Forces of Light to neutralize the negative forces within the planetary energy-field and to stabilize that energy-field and move it towards the Light.

With the coming of the New Avatāra and the new cosmic alignment, this work is not going to be done by just one person because now the crisis is so big that it is affecting the whole planet and all of Mankind. It would be nice if Jesus were to be born again and die for all of our sins so that we wouldn't have to do anything, but that's not going to happen. Now we have to make a choice as a total humanity; every single human being has to make this choice: Are you going to be on the side of the Forces of Light and Evolution that will bring about the planetary rebirth of Mother Earth? Or are you content to sit back and wait and see what happens? You can do that, but then you are playing into the hands of the negative forces that want to keep Humanity in the state of Ignorance and Darkness that we have lived in for hundreds of thousands of years.

The Science of the Spiritual Warrior will help you make an intelligent choice—but it has to be a *choice*, freely embraced because you understand its significance and meaning. The Truth can be presented but it cannot be forced upon anyone. That's why it is so important to understand what needs to be done and put your weight into it and decide, "I am going to be a Warrior of Light!" Not just for your own sake but for the sake of all Humanity and all life on the planet.

The Spiritual Warrior and the Opposition

The romantic novels of the Middle Ages portrayed the Warrior as a knight in shining armour who says farewell to his beloved lady, gallops off to fight in a world of good versus bad and returns home and lives happily ever after. That is the romantic life of the Warrior, but the real life of the Warrior is different. If you are a world messenger, if you work for the Spiritual Hierarchy or work for the Light, you are automatically marked for opposition. As a Spiritual Warrior, a "knight in shining armour" (an armour of Light), it is important to understand and accept the Principle of Opposition:

THE MORE LIGHT YOU SHED AROUND YOU, THE MORE THE OPPOSITION INCREASES AGAINST YOU.

You have to understand that this is not a philosophy but something very real: if you give out a little Light from your inner being, then the opposition is minimal; if you give out more Light the opposition increases; if you radiate a lot of Light, you encounter a lot of opposition.

I will explain *why* and *how* the Opposition can attack you and what's going on in terms of the reality of the Inner Worlds. Every structure exists in duality or polarity. For example, in human society there are male and female; the atom has positively and negatively charged particles; a magnet has opposite poles; where there is good there is bad; where there is light there is darkness. As a Warrior of Light, you have to understand that you will get opposition from the Darkness when you work for the Light. It is a law pervading Reality.

Logically, you could ask: Why is there Opposition? Why would everyone *not* want to work for the Light, to create a glorious, shining planet of Light? Why would people even bother to oppose this idea? Well, they do, and they have been doing it since the times of Lemuria and Atlantis, because the Opposition, the Forces of Darkness, are human beings, elemental entities and angelic hierarchies that are crystallized; that is to say, they want to keep things as they are, unchanged. (Against them are the Forces of Light, which are always moving in an upward evolutionary spiral, creating new expressions, new ideas, new states of being, new states of awareness.) They have not been created by any particular group or organization but have existed for aeons as forces working to keep human consciousness in a state of darkness, unaware of the spiritual dimensions and higher realities.

The Light increases as one ascends through the Inner Planes, so obviously the Opposition wants Humanity to remain in the lower dimensions. That's why I say materialism is dangerous—while people are totally materialistic and happily enjoying a material life they are not receiving the Light or raising their consciousness, and that is exactly what the Opposition wants. If Humanity were to bring the irresistible Light of Nirvāṇa all the way down to this physical dimension, it would annihilate all darkness and opposition, so it is in the interest of the Opposition to keep human consciousness in darkness.

The average person living a normal life just follows along with events, without any understanding of what is happening (in the esoteric sense). History shows governments, cultures and religions falling and rising, and people think that that's just history; in reality, however, that history has been manipulated. As a Spiritual Warrior you understand this manipulation of the negative materialistic forces and oppose it with your Light, and whether or not you are consciously aware that you are shedding Light, you will automatically be opposed. Even if you are a political, religious, artistic or scientific figure who is working to uplift Mankind, you will be opposed. What you call yourself doesn't matter; you are attacked for what you *do*.

I have been observing the struggle between the Light and the Dark, how the opposing forces manifest, since I was a child. To me it is a very real thing, and due to the nature of what I do I have encountered much opposition over the decades. Anyone who tries to regenerate the consciousness of Humanity or the planet has to take it for granted that there will be opposition and understand how it comes and how to deal with it.

Attacks of the Opposition can be:

(a) Physical

(b) Emotional

(c) Mental

(d) Psychic

(e) Against your reputation or your work

When you are a Light worker or a true Spiritual Warrior, the Opposition arranges various things for you to make your life more interesting. Like army generals looking for the weak point in the enemy lines, they look at your total personality (your physical, astral and mental bodies) for possibilities of damaging you on any of those levels, separately or all at once, and they do this from your birth and even before your birth, in the Inner Worlds.

For instance, the Opposition knew that the Christ was going to be a major Light-bringer for the planet, so they wanted to keep Him from coming down through the planes and tried to stop Him on the Astral Plane. After He was born they wanted to kill Him as a child, and all throughout His life the Opposition worked until He was crucified. Avatāras—great Light-bringers like the Buddha and the Christ—are guarded on the Inner Planes by angelic hierarchies during their incarnation process into the Physical World, but once they are born it is difficult for the angels to do anything because at that stage the physical laws apply. Hopefully, a few people understand who these Beings of Light really are and are able to help them in their physical life so that they can carry out their mission.

Now, the attacks can be *physical*: Mahatma Gandhi was shot, the Christ was crucified and millions of followers of the Bahai Faith, including Light-bringers like Bahá'u'lláh and Abdu'l-Bahá, were physically tortured or killed.

The Opposition can also attack you *emotionally*, on the level of your astral body, by sending you tremendous waves of panic in the Astral World. For no apparent reason, you become afraid of life in general or afraid to take any action, so you close yourself down.

And they can attack you *mentally* by influencing your mind, twisting your thoughts or giving you wrong ideas, making you believe that what you are doing is useless or a waste of time. That is a common trick. Your mission in life to help Humanity may be clear to you, but they can throw you off your plan by influencing the mind in such a way that you simply give up on your project. Jesus experienced this a few times. Once He was on a mount looking down on Jerusalem and said, "Oh Jerusalem, Jerusalem, how many times would I have put you together [bring you back into God], and you would not" (MATTHEW 23: 37). He was terribly depressed that all His work was a waste of time, that the people would never really reach out for God.

The Opposition can also attack you *psychically* by using psychic forces against you. For example, I was once attacked on the psychic level by a part of the Opposition that was once located in Thule, Greenland, which was a major centre of Black Magic during Atlantean times. Their attacks can be so powerful and overwhelming that you become paralyzed inside, even though as a Spiritual Warrior you know what is happening, you know that you can be protected through Mantra, that you can invoke the forces of the Christ Hierarchy or the Spiritual Hierarchy. During the Thule attack, I invoked the Christ, the Buddha, the Lord Maitreya and in the end Sanat Kumāra, the great King of Light, and the Opposition finally gave up.

Another way the Opposition can attack is *against your reputation or your work.* They want to destroy your name, the influence you have in the world, the way you are helping society and the work you are doing in your particular field, the work you are doing as a Spiritual Warrior for the world—and they go about it intelligently and systematically.

I have had attacks on all of those levels and sometimes simultaneously. I was once attacked on the physical, emotional, mental and psychic levels in an all-out attack. It was a cleverly organized car accident that paralyzed my whole personality mechanism, and it took many months for my physical, astral and mental bodies to recover and heal.

Once you feel that you are being attacked, on any level or against your reputation or your work, the best thing to do is: accept that you are in a battle condition, that it is part of being a Spiritual Warrior, and then stabilize yourself in the Light and centre yourself in the Heart, which will tell you what you have to do. Sometimes the Heart tells you to do absolutely nothing, to let the storm rage around you until it dies out. Sometimes the Heart tells you to attack or defend as in any war situation.

This is part of the understanding of the life of the Spiritual Warrior. You don't automatically fight like you would normally do if somebody hits you. That's the common human reaction, but not how a Spiritual Warrior does things. Jesus was a Warrior. He was a descendant of King David and belonged to the Jewish warrior class and lived by the Warrior Code. He said "If somebody hits you on the cheek, give him the other cheek also"(MATTHEW 5: 39). This is difficult for the worldly person to understand; the way of the world is to strike back.

The Opposition can work against you through:

(a) Relatives, family, friends

(b) Workmates

(c) Strangers

(d) Invisible forces

(e) Elementals

It is important to understand how the Opposition can attack you at any time, on any level, and one more thing to know is *who* the Opposition can use.

(a) Relatives, family, friends

A favourite way of attacking you is through your relatives, family and friends, in other words, the people who are closest to you. You are most vulnerable to being attacked by those people whom you trust the most, the people right inside your castle, your family home. This may seem illogical but the Opposition doesn't use logic in the way the average human being understands it. They start working on the people in your intimate circle and find a weak point, someone whom they can twist on the emotional, mental or psychic level and make them feel anger towards you. They will do anything that will produce a split or disharmony between you and them, and they keep feeding that disharmony until there is a blow-up. Remember, the Opposition consists of intelligent beings and forces and they have an understanding of your condition and know how to work on you.

(b) Workmates

Workmates are people you associate with from day to day either in a physical workplace or as part of your social networking. The Opposition can inspire one of those people to hate you and then bring in other workmates to create a whole army of people against you.

(c) Strangers

Although you have no association with strangers, the Opposition can stir up somebody against you who may be emotionally, mentally or psychically weak, until they go berserk. For example, John Lennon was shot by a stranger. He was generating positive energy and was a force for change, so the Opposition found a weak person to shoot him. Just because you don't know someone does not mean that they can't be inspired to work against you. The Opposition can work on anybody and sometimes the best agent is a stranger who has a certain weakness they can exploit.

(d) Invisible forces

This is on a more subtle level, but the Opposition can channel invisible forces against you. These are not intelligent beings but natural forces, usually negative forces so overwhelmingly powerful that they make you endanger your life, like jump off a cliff or drive your car into a tree. The use of invisible forces is a favourite of the Opposition because it's something you don't expect, and these forces can cause physical death, emotional instability, insanity or an overwhelming wave of depression.

(e) Elementals

Another common way to attack a Warrior of Light is by using elementals. Elemental beings are innocent creatures in the invisible worlds (the etheric-physical dimensions and the Astral World). They are much like animals—they have no rational mind and are instinctual, functioning according to certain naturally established patterns. So if an opposing force puts pressure on them to attack you, they will; they can't use logic to figure out that it is not a good idea. You can be attacked by air elementals (pressure), fire elementals (burning) and water elementals (drowning), and they can attack in large numbers.

Whether you want to be a Spiritual Warrior or not, you will encounter opposition if you are working to benefit Humanity or to increase the Light on this planet. Because of the planetary crisis, the Opposition is growing stronger and they will fight you tooth and nail. You have to understand this and accept it as the Law of Nature. So when you feel an attack, centre in the Heart and take as much time as you need to tune into what the Heart wants, because the Heart understands the situation completely. When you come out you will know exactly what to do.

PRACTICE

The Warrior Mantra

RĀM RĀMĀYA NAMAHA

Intoning the Warrior Mantra will help to increase the Divine Light-energy of the Warrior within you. Unlike the previous technique of *Surrendering the Ego to the Heart*, which is a passive, stabilizing meditation, the Warrior Mantra is an active meditation, working with the Light-force to *project* the energy and to *expand* your Light-force. It throws the Light outside of you and creates a shield of Light around you. First intone the Mantra aloud, then intone it mentally (internally and silently).[7]

---

[7] An audio file demonstrating the intonation of this mantra can be found at www.planetary-transformation.org/mantrarepetition

THE WAY OF COSMIC VISION

The Second Gate, the Way of Cosmic Vision, has to do with Light, and I want to tell you about the Light and how we use it to enhance our spiritual evolution on the individual level, the group level and the planetary level.

We'll start with this magical Mantra, which is a statement directly from Cosmic Consciousness:

THE CREATIVE LIGHT SHINES THROUGH ALL CREATION TO ACCOMPLISH ITS PERFECT WORK.

There are two aspects of Light: the *Fundamental Clear Light*, which is the Original Field of Light, the Divine Mind itself, and which is always shining intensely bright, always stable and unchanging; and the *Creative Light*, which descends to accomplish its perfect work, in other words, to bring Creation to the perfection of the Original Light. The Fundamental Clear Light is what the Buddhists call Nirvāṇa or what Jesus called the Original Kingdom or what in Kabbalah is called the *White Brilliance of the Supreme Crown*. It is the root of the Cosmos, the foundation of all things, and some part of that clear, brilliant Light becomes the Creative Light, which then creates the Inner Worlds and the Physical World.

What we call *matter* is really Light at its slowest vibration, and the same Light exists through the Inner Planes as an ever-increasing frequency of Vibration right up to the Fundamental Clear Light, which is so fast that it appears to be not moving at all. The scientific idea of light involves only a fraction of the reality of Light, so you have to expand your understanding of Light beyond how it is perceived by science.

Now, the Creative Light has been shining through all Creation since the beginning of Creation and it will be there until the end, but—and this is a big but—*we do not perceive it.* And that's where the Way of Cosmic Vision comes in, because it is about understanding the Light structure of the Universe, understanding how the Light works and what its function is in the Cosmos. Essential to understanding the Way of Cosmic Vision is the realization that the Light is not just the source of physical light to make everything look nice or show how radiant God is. No, it is Cosmic Intelligence, the Cosmic Mind of God, and it has a purpose: to accomplish its perfect work.

In my book *Planetary Transformation* I mentioned that Planet Earth is going through a major change, which is not due solely to the movements of our planet and Solar System through the zodiacal signs or into a different part of our galaxy but to something more profound: the *coming* of the Light. But if the Creative Light has always been there, what does it mean that it is coming? It means that although the Creative Light has always been shining since the foundation of the Universe, at certain cyclical times it becomes more active in certain places, according to some cosmic design, in some Solar System or other or on a planet within this Solar System or in the life of our Mother, the Planetary Logos, or our Father, the Solar Logos.

Finally, after millions of years, the Creative Light is putting attention on our planet, and this is why there are big changes coming. The Light has been focusing on our planet since the time of Christ, when it became active in the higher realms, and it has been steadily increasing, especially since 1875, as it stimulated the lower realms—first the Mental World, then the Astral World and finally the Physical World. The Light is pressing down on this planet, but it is not going to change us without our permission, because of our free will. Free will means that to evolve you have to be consciously involved in your evolution. So the problem lies with us: we need to do something about ourselves, to remove the obstacles and develop the ability to perceive the Light and consciously use it. We have to understand our position in life, our stature and dignity as human beings, and use our free will to accomplish the perfect work.

So how are we going to accomplish this perfect work? Since the Second Gate is the Way of Cosmic Vision, we have to open the Third-Eye Centre and be able to see or sense the Light, even if we can only sense the energy of it. And then we have to choose to use it, to cooperate consciously and intelligently with the Divine Plan. Then the Light, *through us*, will accomplish its perfect work with our cooperation.

Light is Sattva—Purity and Harmony

The Universe has three primary qualities: RAJAS, intense activity; TAMAS, non-activity; and SATTVA, purity and harmony. These qualities or forces are always in conflict on the Physical Plane, where there always exists the desire to be active and busy and the desire to relax and do nothing. Our whole society is based upon those two qualities because human beings do everything through either Rajas (activity, with everything winding up to a point where a nervous breakdown can be the end result) or Tamas (inactivity, with everything winding down to a point of nothingness where depression or suicide can be the end result). The basic problem of human society is that it exists between the extremes of these two qualities and very few people have the quality of Sattva—purity and harmony.

Purity in this sense is not about being a vegetarian or following a specific lifestyle; it refers to having a higher frequency of vibration compared with that at which matter normally vibrates. Sattva brings balance and harmony between the opposite polarities of Rajas and Tamas and imparts the sensation of wellness and harmony, like champagne fizzing inside you or like the buzz of a high-frequency vibration. These extreme forces are within every person on this planet in different degrees, and the problems of human relationship will not go away until we, as a community, live in Sattva, in the Light. Therefore, a fundamental transformation of human society is needed.

Light and the Changing of Relationships and Social Structures

It is easier to understand the inner workings and functions of the Light if we can relate our understanding to how it affects us on the physical level, although the real function and esoteric significance of Light is impersonal and far beyond the personality. In relationships, on the level of individuals and society, you will notice the two opposing forces of Rajas and Tamas at work. Some people have more of the Tamas energy while others have more of the Rajas energy, and some have them malfunctioning in varying degrees. Due to the imbalance of those forces people continually fight, trying to adjust those qualities. The Tamasic person wants to make the other person Tamasic and the Rajasic person wants to make the other person Rajasic. So two malfunctioning personalities are trying to live in harmony and peace—qualities they don't have.

When this is applied to millions of people, then we have societies where people live in total disharmony, where the entire population is continually generating wrong energy, and violence and corruption pervade the whole society. Of course, social workers, psychologists and politicians try to make up rules on how people should behave, *without being in the state of harmony themselves*, so their ideas on how society should function remain as ideas only; there is no fundamental change in the nature of human beings because rules and ideas do not change people *internally*.

It's important to understand that if you want to change something, first change yourself. Don't worry about the imperfections of other people; that is not your job. Once you have actually changed yourself, that in itself is the blessing, that in itself will alter your environment, and the people around you will change according to their ability to pick up your vibration. If you have the right kind of vibration, the right kind of energy (which is basically Sattvic energy), people will want that energy. Human society appreciates the quality of Sattva and wants it but doesn't know where to get it.

This is where the Science of Light comes in. We know that the basic qualities of Light on the physical level are purity, harmony, peace, integrity, wholeness, completeness. You may be violent, angry, irritated or overworking to the point of collapse, with an imbalance of Rajas. Conversely, you may be lazy and inactive and expect somebody else, the government or the welfare system, to look after you, which means you have too much Tamasic energy. What if you awaken the Light Principle inside you? The Light of the Soul, the Light of the Spirit and the Light of God are the same one Light on different levels, and when that principle is awakened within you, your imbalance becomes harmonized and you become filled with Light and the quality of Sattva.

The Light will balance the two opposing forces of Rajas and Tamas inside you and you will react positively to whatever happens in your environment. Otherwise, you will react like others normally do: anger for anger, violence for violence, laziness for laziness; the way society normally functions. But if you are in the state of Sattva you will be more loving, gentle and self-controlled, no matter what others may do, because you are in the state of harmony and understand that others are acting from an imbalance of human nature. The Light will balance your physical body, your emotional nature and your mind nature, and the more Light you have inside you, the more you will radiate out that balance and harmony. It is you yourself who are the *transforming* reality. Because you have transformed yourself, you transform your environment; you become an intermediary between the Light and human society. You don't have to think about it; it's just automatic.

One person in a state of harmony will have a calming effect on the environment. What if couples did this Light Work? Their relationship would change a hundred percent. Both of them would be calm and harmonized, and what is more, the positive vibration in both of them would increase in a multidimensional way: two persons with the Sattva quality produce a Light-radiation that is tenfold the radiation of one person. Now what if you have a whole group of such people? The group would generate a field of Light that would spread out and produce the state of Sattva in the larger environment. People would feel less aggressive, plants would grow better, the angels would dance in Heaven—the whole of Creation would be literally filled with harmony.

As I mentioned before, the Avatāra is already here within the Solar System, beaming the Light into the planetary structure like a lens, but the Avatāra cannot come and knock everybody on the head one by one. Society has to be changed by the Light-force itself, so we have to have carriers of the Light, people who emanate that Light-force within society. And to have people emanating the Light, they have to first attain the Light themselves. You can't say somebody else will do it. The process of change moves from you (the individual) to the group to the planet. So if we have increasingly more numbers of human beings working with the Light-force, *consciously, intelligently*, they will naturally emanate a larger frequency of the Light and therefore impact on society. This is exactly how Light changes the social structure.

Unfortunately, because of ignorance and the lack of Enlightenment on this planet, people are not able to perceive the Light, not able to understand the tremendous opportunity that is available to us at this time.

The materialistic philosophy of life is that this *physical* body is the only true self and this *physical* world we see is the only reality. Consequently, every aspect of society is materialistic—science, philosophy, art, psychology, politics—and the material energy stream, with billions of people immersed in it, is the overwhelmingly predominant energy stream of this planet. Many people are so unaware of anything beyond the physical body that even simple concepts such as the mind and emotions existing apart from the body are weird ideas. Everyone works on this physical plane for this physical plane existence, unaware of the inner dimensions, the inner realities. Humankind is trapped in Darkness.

The materialistic philosophy of life is not correct and it is not the purpose of existence. Already two thousand years ago the Christ understood how society, including the so-called religious authorities, was degenerate and materialistic. He was walking in the fields with his disciples and saw that there were two or three people cutting the ripened wheat and He said, "The harvest is ready, but the harvesters are few" (MATTHEW 9: 37). The situation is the same today, if not worse. This planet is ready for a spiritual harvest but those who are able to do it are so few in number.

The Avatāra is a tremendous Light-force which, let loose on the planet, will change every country and every race, provided that there is sufficient Light penetrating the human structure. This is *the* solution for society's problems. Philosophers for thousands of years have been trying to make rules for how society should be, but it is not ideas that will change society. It is something else: a real force, a real energy that works *inside* people. Laws like you shall not kill and you shall not steal are good ideas, but people still kill and steal. The Light-force equalizes the disharmony inside people and when they attain harmony they automatically become good. It's automatic because they would feel bad otherwise. When you have the Light working inside you, you cannot murder a person; it just wouldn't feel right. The Light itself will make you feel completely out of tune whenever you do something wrong. The Light gives you the standard, and it's not a human standard, a human law; it's the Universal Law of Creation, the ultimate law, the ultimate reference point for all existence.

The best way you can help is to work with this Light, because with a sufficient number of people this planet will be transformed into a planet of Light. And then all our human social problems will disappear. Violence will disappear, wars will disappear, sicknesses will disappear and Mother Nature herself will calm down. It may be hard to understand but Mother Nature is simply reacting to seven billion people pounding the atmosphere of the planet with all kinds of negative emotional and mental forces that keep accumulating in the Inner Worlds like a tremendous ocean of dark and gooey energy. Well, Mother Earth wants to shake off that energy—anybody would! And in the end She'll get rid of all Humanity if we don't do the right thing. We have to start changing the way we do things on this planet; Mother Earth will not put up with us for too long.

Working with the Light—the GĀYATRĪ MANTRA

At this stage, we need to reconnect to our spiritual reality, our own divine natures, all the amazing possibilities that there are in the Cosmos. Now we have to try to counter the effects of materialism and negative energy as much as possible by working intelligently with a powerful force of the Light—the GĀYATRĪ MANTRA.

The Gāyatrī Mantra originated thousands of years ago, when a great Seer attained a high degree of Enlightenment, a high degree of Oneness with the Solar Logos. In the state of Cosmic Consciousness, the Intelligence within that great Sage wished for a way that others could experience what he was experiencing and immediately the answer came forth in the mantric syllables known as the Gāyatrī Mantra. When he returned from that deep state of spiritual trance, he began giving the Mantra to his own pupils, who progressed to attain union with the Solar Logos, the Divine Light.

So we know that there is something we can use whereby the Divine Light will respond to us and intelligently know that we are invoking it and wanting to work with it to accomplish its perfect work. If we think, as a philosopher would, that we can just ask the Light to come and automatically transform the world, it won't. Thinking has no effect on it at all because the Light is supremely intelligent and it has to work in a certain way. And that way, that technique of intelligently working with the Light, is the Gāyatrī Mantra. When we work with the Gāyatrī, we are invoking *the Light that shines through all Creation*. We are making a conscious decision to work with the Light because it is a field of Absolute Intelligence and therefore working with it will make *our* intelligence absolute. As you become the Light you become omnipresent, omnipotent and omniscient, because the Light is omnipresent, omnipotent and omniscient.

The Gāyatrī Mantra is the Way of Cosmic Vision. This has been ordained for thousands of years and of course in the olden days it was kept secret because the Gurus and Seers would only give it to those who were ready to work with the Light. In India, the Gāyatrī was not allowed to be uttered by anyone other than the priest class, the upper levels of the Brahman class, so the ordinary person on the street was not allowed to even know about it. Over the past six to eight thousand years, however, the priests began to include the Gāyatrī in many daily rituals, repeating it many times a day, and over time they lost the understanding of its true purpose and meaning, thinking of it as just a nice prayer that was part of their ceremonies and rituals.

THE GĀYATRĪ MANTRA IS THE SPEECH OF GOD, THE SONG OF GOD, AN INVOCATION TO THE LIGHT THAT THE LIGHT ITSELF CREATED FOR US.

The word Gāyatrī literally means the "Song of God", and because it is a divine song, the Gāyatrī Mantra is motivated by Divinity. *It is an invocation to the Light that the Light Itself created for us.* In all its forms, it has a certain inner rhythm, an inner pattern not produced externally by a musician. Nowadays in India many musicians make songs about the Gāyatrī or use the Mantra to make songs or melodies, but these are obviously mentally, or externally, created; they're not an impulse from within. I received the Gāyatrī from within; I did not hear it externally. Only when you internally receive a mantra can you understand that there is a divine impulse inherent in the structure of the mantra itself—a divine impulse that is the *way* the Divine Light works.

When a Guru invokes the Gāyatrī, a huge, solid beam of Light comes from the centre of the Sun (regardless of where the Earth is in relation to the Sun) and goes through the Guru's Heart and then radiates out to each person present. The Light divides itself evenly depending on the number of people present—no more, no less—and then each of those rays divides into two, touching the Third Eye and Heart Centres of each person simultaneously. If you could see this happening, just once, you would be totally amazed at how intelligent the Light of God is! It does not waste one iota of energy; it divides itself evenly to touch the exact number of people, whether there be a few or thousands.

After some repetition of the Mantra there begins a huge circulation of the Light, which then speeds up and starts ascending as a vast energy-field, rising through the astral, mental, causal and Buddhic dimensions. When it reaches a certain point in Inner Space, it explodes, producing a response, a downpour of energy from the Buddhic and Nirvāṇic dimensions that is literally like a tidal wave flooding the three lower dimensions. That is the magic of the Light, and that is how we work with the Light to accomplish its perfect work. We are the work of the Light, so when we work with the Light it will recreate us towards perfection, towards the divine image we should be.

When we recreate ourselves we also recreate the world because everything in Nature is interconnected, so we impact on the whole world according to whatever we become. By working with the Light, we can try to overcome some of the dense, heavy vibration materialism produces on this planet so that the Light can do its perfect work of purifying the planet and turning it into a field of Light. This time it is possible for that to happen; but whether it happens depends on whether human beings are able to work with the Light within the next 300 years. This world can become one of the shining planets of Light with a completely new civilization, a civilization not based on matter but Light. People will be able to see, hear and understand that which is not possible for them to perceive at this stage. We will be like Christs and Buddhas walking on the Earth, *if* we have sufficient numbers of people to spread this Knowledge and Wisdom and do this Work.

The Words of the Gāyatrī Mantra and Their Meaning

ŌM BHŪR BHUVAH SVAHA
ŌM TAT SAVITUR VARENYAM
BHARGO DEVASYA DHĪMAHI
DHIYO YO NAH PRACHODAYĀT
ŌM

Glory be to you, Solar Logos.
Glory be to you, Spiritual Sun.
In you we live, move and have our Being,
In the Light of our Lord, the Sun.

The above translation is the essence behind the Gāyatrī, not a literal translation. The following is a word-by-word translation of the Sanskrit so that when you practise it you will understand the meaning of each word and be aware of what you are invoking.

ŌM *The Primordial Reality*, the Oneness, the Unity of all things, or the Unity-Field—not the "unified field" of science. The scientific term implies that all the many energies have been put together or unified into one field, but that is incorrect. The One Field existed before everything else; it doesn't need unification. Ōm invokes the state of Unity, where the Creative Light is still a single Ocean of Reality.

BHŪR *The Physical World.*

BHUVAH *The Astral World, the After-Death World.*

SVAHA *The Heaven Worlds (Mental World).*

In this first line, we are invoking the Sounding-Light, the Creative-Light Vibration, to come down into the Physical World, the Astral World and the Mental World (which includes the Heaven Worlds). There are other forms of the Gāyatrī Mantra that invoke the Light in the higher dimensions (the Buddhic, Nirvāṇic and Paranirvāṇic dimensions), but this is the basic form that invokes the Light into the lower worlds of Creation, where human beings function.

TAT *That*

SAVITUR *The Divine Sun.* The Sanskrit word SAVITUR refers to the Solar Logos, the Creative Intelligence within the Sun; the great ĪŚVARA, the ruler of our Solar System, which has seventy-two planets—twelve visible and sixty invisible planets—within its psychic aura.

VARENYAṀ *We worship.* The esoteric meaning is that we not only worship the Divine Sun but are *empowered* to worship the Divine Sun because of our initiation into the Gāyatrī Mantra. *That Divine Sun, we (are empowered to) worship.*

BHARGO *The Light, the Radiance, the Glory.*

DEVASYA *Of God.*

DHĪMAHI *We contemplate, we see.* We are on the Way of Cosmic Vision, the Way of the Divine Light, the Divine Radiance, the Light of God.

DHIYO From DHĪ, which in Sanskrit dictionaries is normally translated as "intelligence", "mind" or "consciousness" but esoterically means the "spiritual faculty", the faculty that enables Cosmic Vision.

YO NAH *Our.*

PRACHODAYĀT *Stimulate, increase, awaken* (our Cosmic Vision).

ŌṀ *Return to Unity.*

We are asking the Creative Light to come down to us, to the Physical, Astral and Mental Worlds, and awaken our faculty of Cosmic Vision—not the vision but the *faculty* of it. Why? Because that faculty is dormant in the average person, and because when our faculty of Cosmic Vision is awakened we are on a different plane of existence. Cosmic Vision is awakened according to three possibilities: in the Third-Eye Cakra; in the Third-Eye Cakra in combination with the Heart Cakra; and in the Third-Eye Cakra in combination with the Crown Cakra. (The Sanskrit word Cakra, pronounced *chakra*, means "wheel of fire" and refers to an energy centre.)

If Cosmic Vision is awakened only in your Third-Eye Centre, you will have limited vision, depending on how your system works: if it opens to the etheric dimensions of the Physical World, you will see ethereal forms; if it opens to the Astral World, you will see the inhabitants of the Astral World—people who have died, those who are coming into incarnation, various elemental beings; and if it opens to the Mental World, you will see the auras and thoughts of people, you will see angels and Devas and you will be able to foretell the future. But when Cosmic Vision awakens in the Third-Eye Cakra and it links up with the Heart Cakra, you acquire the vision of the Kingdom of God within you and you know how you relate to the Divinity Within; you perceive the Deity, how God exists outside of you in the Cosmos, the whole dynamic Cosmic Reality.

We do not specify the way in which we experience the Supernatural Reality; the Light will come to us according to our readiness, our evolutionary development and our dedication to and understanding of the Path. It is not the same for everybody. For instance, if you are a psychic person, you will see the lower, middle or higher Astral World, which is a limited vision called *clairvoyance*. If you are a mystical or devotional person, the Light will most likely awaken your Heart Centre and the awareness of the Divinity inside you. If you are a scientific person or a "knower" (JÑĀNI in Sanskrit), it will reveal a vision of the entire Cosmos and how the Cosmos functions on the inner dimensions.

Now that the meanings of the individual words of the Gāyatrī have been explained, we'll take each line separately and go a little deeper into the meaning of the Mantra so that you can be aware of the meaning while you are invoking this beautiful gift of the Light.

ŌM BHŪR BHUVAH SVAHA

Here we first invoke the Unity-Field, the Ocean of Oneness (Ōm) and then break the single field of Unity into three (BHŪR BHUVAH SVAHA) so that the Light can differentiate itself and become active in the physical, astral and mental dimensions.

ŌM TAT SAVITUR VARENYAM

In this line dwells the true magic of the Gāyatrī. Through the rite of Initiation, through the transference of energy from Guru to disciple, we are *entitled* and *empowered* to worship that Divine Light, the Spiritual Sun, the Solar Logos. It is an entitlement because the transmission of the Divine Light has been properly received from the Guru. This is the secret that the priestcraft of India has forgotten.

When we bring down the Light into the Three Worlds, it changes our whole perception of reality, our vibration, our attitude toward existence. It is a tremendous service to the world because the Light cannot be contained only within an individual or a group; it has to flood out to the entire planet. We become open gates, or doorways, to that Light so it can accomplish its perfect work of transformation and rejuvenation of individuals, groups and the whole planet.

The worship of the Sun is the most direct worship of God. It is not the worship of some inanimate object in the sky. Just as your physical body is only the outermost layer of you as a spiritual being, the physical Sun and the physical Solar System are the outermost part of the physical body of the Spiritual Sun, or Solar Logos. The Solar Logos is a being, just as you and I are beings, but He is infinitely more vast and glorious than we are. In the Old Testament it is said that God created us in His image. We are miniature suns existing as multidimensional beings in the same way that the Solar Logos is a multidimensional being but on a vast cosmic scale, a Cosmic Intelligence at a very high level of cosmic-evolutionary attainment. Our Solar Logos is an individualized consciousness—alive, intelligent, living in Cosmic Space and reflecting God's Divinity, Absolute Intelligence, Love, Light and Life.

The Solar Logos is literally the God "in whom we live, move and have our being" (ACTS 17: 28). We are living *in* God; that is, we are living *in* the Sun, and every planet in our Solar System, visible and invisible, is living in the vast, pulsating energy of His auric field on every layer of Creation.

BHARGO DEVASYA DHĪMAHI

We are telling the Divine Light, the All-Creative Light of the Deity (BHARGO DEVASYA), that we want to attain Cosmic Vision through contemplation (DHĪMAHI) of that Divine Light.

DHIYO YO NAH PRACHODAYĀT

Here we ask the Divine Being within the Sun to stimulate and awaken our faculty of Cosmic Vision. Religious people often pray to God for physical things but we are not asking for any material benefits; we are simply asking for the power of Cosmic Vision, the greatest gift we could ask from the Deity because with Cosmic Vision we can become omniscient, omnipotent and omnipresent. This is the highest understanding of true religion; this is why the Gāyatrī is such an incredibly sacred mantra.

Ōṁ

The final Ōṁ resolves everything back into the state of Unity. We say that we now have Cosmic Vision and all is back to the unconditional state of Oneness.

In the Bible, Christ said, "Let your Light so shine before man that they may see your good works and glorify your Father in Heaven" (MATTHEW 5: 16). Christ taught the Gāyatrī to his disciples in Aramaic, and after they were initiated and working with the Light, He told them to use their Third Eye to get the Light out into the world: *Let your Light so shine before Mankind.* The Third-Eye Centre is the directing agency for the Light and you first have to awaken it and then learn to channel the Light through the Third Eye so that you can direct and work with the Light intelligently, *that they may see your good works.* The *good works* refers to the magic of the Light, the transforming power of the Light, and when people realize this they will *glorify the Father in Heaven.* In Biblical times, the word *Heaven* meant the Inner Space, the totality of the invisible Reality.

Unveiling the Hidden Worlds

The following statement is both a profound teaching and a practical technique; that is, if you can grasp it and put it into practice it will take you to Enlightenment straight away:

CONCENTRATION ON THE AWAKENED LIGHT WILL UNVEIL THE HIDDEN WORLDS—THE WAY OF COSMIC VISION.

The Esoteric Science is a science like any other. Science is based on the idea that you can prove something by experiment, and if other people do the same experiment they get the same results. Well, the Esoteric Science is exactly like that: we prove something by experiment and everybody who does the experiment properly will get the same results. To open the Second Gate, the Way of Cosmic Vision, all you have to do is first awaken the Light and then concentrate on it. And the result? You will see the Hidden Worlds. It's as simple as that. Regardless of your religion, politics or background—even if you are a materialist who does not believe that there are hidden worlds!—the Light will automatically unveil the Hidden Worlds to you, if you do the right work under the right conditions.

We mentioned previously that the Light is already there, shining within all Creation and within you too, right within your physical body, your emotional nature and your mind—not to mention, of course, your Soul, which is made of Light. The Light is essentially within everything, all of the time. But knowing that it's there, in itself, doesn't do anything because the human mechanism is not geared to perceive the Light on the physical level, in the same way as it is incapable of *hearing* the higher Sound-Vibration or *sensing* the Presence of the Deity internally or externally. Once you understand that, you know that you have to *do* something, and that something is: awakening the Light.

To awaken the Light you have to practise certain techniques that awaken the Light, like the Gāyatrī Mantra[8] or a Third-Eye meditation like Ōṁ Namo Ōṁ Namah[9]. The most superior technique is the Gāyatrī, because the Gāyatrī itself is Light. When you intone the Gāyatrī the Light particles inside you become active—so active, eventually, that you can't help seeing the Light. Even if you are psychically blind, you will feel its vibration and know it's there. The Third Eye sees even when it is asleep or closed, but that *seeing* we call "sensing". It's like being in a dark room: you can't see objects or people in the room but you can sense them. So when you start working with the Light, you will *sense* the Light, sense that it is becoming bright inside you or brightening up the room. Then there comes a point when you can actually see flickering sparks of Light in the Third Eye. Later on, those sparks of Light become steady and you can see a soft light like moonlight.

Once you see a light, whether it's sparks of light or a little candle flame or just a soft light, you should start concentrating on it. Simply gaze at it steadily. Don't try to change it or do anything to it; don't try to grab it with your ego because if you use your willpower it will disappear. After a while the light will become steady and you will see a shimmering field of light either around you or inside you, in the Third Eye. It could be a huge field of light or a little one, but once it becomes steady keep concentrating on it. And then suddenly, as if a veil or dark cloth has been torn off your eyes, you begin to see into the Inner Worlds.

When the Third Eye first opens it may reveal the etheric-physical dimensions, which are the four regions, or subplanes, of the Physical World that we normally don't see. Then, you may see the translucent

---

[8] See the Gāyatrī Mantra Meditation on page 96.
[9] See "Mantra Repetition in the Third-Eye Centre" on page 157.

bodies of angels in front of you or seas of energies inside and around you. Later you may see the astral dimensions and then the causal dimensions and the Buddhic dimensions. You will know which dimension you are seeing by the type of things you see: if you see shapes, fluidic objects and movement of fluidic matter, then it is the Astral World; if you see beautiful cities made of gold, rubies and diamonds and exquisite shapes of trees and plants, you are in the Mind World; if you see shimmering energy-fields, you are in the Causal World; if you see the soft light of the moon permeating all of Creation, you are in the Buddhic World; and if you see a bright, overpowering light, the White Brilliance, then you are in the Nirvāṇic World.

You cannot control which of the Hidden Worlds will be unveiled to you. This is hard for the human ego because the human ego says, "I want this"; otherwise it wouldn't be an ego. But unfortunately in the spiritual world *I want* gets you nowhere. In the spiritual world you *aspire*, you are inflamed with a longing for the Reality you know is there, and that longing has to be totally innocent, totally selfless. Once you attain the right attitude, the Hidden Worlds open because they have been there all the time; something takes away the veil and you just *see*.

Nothing you do can be contained within yourself, so when you achieve something it is communicated to your group and then the worldwide community. For example, when the Buddha attained Nirvāṇa, after a tremendous amount of self-discipline and meditation, His Third Eye opened to astral, causal, Buddhic and finally Nirvāṇic Vision, and because of that there was a major planetary transformation. Similarly, when the Christ first contacted the field of Universal Love, His achievement had a transforming effect on the planet. In other words, when a person reaches a higher level of consciousness it rebounds on the planet depending on the degree of attainment. Because the Buddha and the Christ had high degrees of attainment, the Energy-Vibration they put out was immense and affected the whole planet.

So when you begin to see or sense the Light, it will rebound on your consciousness, on the consciousness of the people around you and to a certain measure on the planet itself. You are part of a community, part of all Creation, and what you experience is not just for yourself; it doesn't work that way. This is why it is important that you work consciously because you are really working for something greater than yourself. It's like the roots of a tree. If a particular root thinks it's getting water for itself it would be deluded; it gets water for the whole tree—trunk, branches and leaves. The sooner you understand this, the sooner you can expand your vision and get behind this Work. At the moment, it is an absolute necessity that the Light impacts the planet.

Prerequisites for the Way of Cosmic Vision

For the First Gate we described five qualities that must be developed in order to follow the Way of the Spiritual Warrior. Similarly, for the Way of Cosmic Vision there are also requirements or rules to practise if you want to succeed on this particular Path.

THE WAY OF COSMIC VISION INVOLVES PURPOSE, DIREC-TION, COMMITMENT AND THE PRACTICAL APPLICATION OF KNOWLEDGE.

The first of these requirements is *purpose*. You have to understand that life is not meaningless and without purpose. Many materialistic philosophers teach the idea of a meaningless existence, and the sciences teach that life is haphazard, it just happens to be the way it is, it has no particular purpose. So first you have to understand that life has a purpose and meaning, and then you have to ask yourself, what is my purpose? Of course, the highest purpose is to develop Cosmic Vision. What else could you do?

The next step is to decide on your *direction;* it's not enough to have a purpose if you don't know where you're going or what you're going to do. Without direction, people try all kinds of things: they join the Hare Krishnas for six months and then some other group for two months; they go from one thing to another, totally lost in life. So you have to have at least a vision of the direction towards the highest goal in life, and you have to have that vision from day one. You have to have your direction and an understanding of life, which you can get through knowledge of the Nine Gates, especially the Second Gate, Cosmic Vision, which is about *cosmic knowledge*—omnipotence, omniscience, omnipresence.

At the next stage you have to have *commitment.* This is where many people fail. They meditate for two days and then they get sidetracked and do something else, and then they remember a year later that they were given a mantra and maybe they should practise it. In other words, once you have a clear direction of where you are going, then you have to commit yourself to it. If your house is washed away by a flood, you could say, "I'm not going to do my meditation today because I have to look after my house." Actually, when you are really committed you will meditate even if your house is being carried away by a flood. In other words, commitment is total, one hundred percent. Nothing will shake you off the Path—not death or sickness or natural disaster; not your wife, your husband, your child, your boss. Nobody. If they do, you are not committed.

People always think that being married and having children is a hindrance to being on the Path, but it isn't. If you decide today that you're going to liberate yourself in this lifetime, that you're going to attain a higher consciousness and understand the mystery of Life in this lifetime, you work at it twenty-four hours a day. It's in the back of your head all the time, a loud scream inside you that that's what you have to do. And then *nothing* will come between you and your commitment. You can still look after your kids, still go to work, still look after all the physical necessities. They won't be obstacles because the commitment is solid and stable inside you.

Commitment is an energy, an interior understanding that you are on the Path, wherever you happen to be, whether riding on a train or flying in an aeroplane or walking in the Gobi Desert. Meditation techniques are part of the expression of that commitment, how you express that commitment, but they are not the commitment itself. The commitment is a transformation inside you, what the Ancients used to call "being reborn"—reborn from the human state into a divine condition. You understand that *this* is your life, what you have to do no matter what the outer circumstances are. And the outer circumstances are actually part of that journey; they move along with you.

The next thing is the *practical application of knowledge*. This is another stage where people fail. They learn about spiritual things, but they don't apply them. For example, people read beautiful scriptures like the New Testament, the Bhagavad-Gītā, the Koran, the Upanishads, the Jewish scriptures and think what amazing stuff—and that's where it stays. There's no practical application of the knowledge. To attain the Way of Cosmic Vision, you have to apply your knowledge. In this particular Gate, we work with the GĀYATRĪ MANTRA to generate the Light inside and distribute it outside. This is the practical application and without it you won't get anywhere, even if you are sincerely committed and have a purpose and direction. Everything is there, but because you don't apply the knowledge you get absolutely nowhere. This is the law of the spiritual world. It's the law of the material world, also. If you want to become a ballerina, it's not enough to read books about the theories of ballet. That's why all knowledge has a practical application; otherwise it's just ideas.

So if you want to follow the way of Cosmic Vision, you need to understand your purpose and direction, have a commitment and apply your knowledge.

PRACTICE

Gāyatrī Mantra Meditation

I will explain how to meditate on the Gāyatrī Mantra in the Third Eye, using the Gāyatrī Root Mantra, which is the easiest form of the Mantra to use.

ŌṀ Bhūr Bhuvah Svaha
ŌṀ Tat Savitur VarenyaṀ
Bhargo Devasya Dhīmahi
Dhiyo Yo Nah Prachodayāt
ŌṀ

The way to meditate on the Mantra is to repeat it slowly and tune into how the energy stream, the subtle Sound-Vibration of the Mantra, pulsates within you. If you do it correctly it will tell you how long any syllable or word or the gap between words should be, and how the energy ends at one line and restarts at the next line, because each of the five lines is an energy-reality that has a beginning and an end. Intoning the first ŌṀ produces a stillness from which you will know how long the gap before the next word should be, and so on. This is where you need to use the Feminine Mind, or the Intuitive Mind, to feel if the Mantric Energy flows in harmony with your inner being.

There are three ways to meditate on this Mantra: with your attention focused in the Heart Centre, in the Third-Eye Centre or in the Crown Centre. The quality of the Light, and how the Light appears, differs in each of those centres. At this time we are focusing the Mantra in the

Third Eye because we want to awaken the awareness of the Light in the Third Eye and send the Light out from there. The first stage of working with the Light is to generate it in the Third-Eye Centre and then sense the Light going out of you. Later you learn how to control it and use it for various purposes from healing to having direct knowledge about all kinds of things. There are hundreds of ways of using the Light but all of that comes later; first you have to do the foundation work.

What you do is, completely relax, forget about everything in the world, think of the Light and repeat the Mantra with your attention focused in the Third-Eye Centre. If you find the whole Mantra too difficult to remember, just intone the Ōṁ sound, which alone can take you to the Light because it is the essence of the Light.[10]

[10] Because of its sacred nature, the Gāyatrī Mantra must be received by direct transmission from a Teacher. Accordingly, no audio file giving the intonation of the Mantra has been provided. If you feel moved to receive the Mantra through the proper channels, you can start the process by going to the Web site of our Spiritual School: www.planetary-transformation.org (Ed.)

About This Technique

The first stage of this meditation involves being able to stay focused in the Third-Eye Centre. Unfortunately, this region of the brain, the front part of your head, is your normal, logical mind (the subconscious mind is at the back of the head and the Superconscious Mind is in the middle area). Since your normal mind is always busy and you need to focus there, there will be a struggle between your busy mind and your ability to concentrate. So just persevere until the energy of the Mantra pacifies your busy mind. It is better to meditate for a short period of time with concentration, without the distraction of your busy thoughts, than to try and meditate for hours while your mind is active.

*****

Scientists are not aware of Inner Space. In Sanskrit, Cidākāśa means "Consciousness-Space"; Consciousness is Space, and Space is Consciousness. The Yogīs knew that Consciousness is multidimensional—it works in physical space and astral, mental and causal space and beyond. Within us there are many layers of Cidākāśa, and at the deeper levels we discover that Space is actually a multidimensional reality and what we know as physical space is only the surface reality.

In the first explorations of Inner Space you may see stars or sparks of Light, and then suddenly something like an eye, an eye within a triangle, a starburst or a gate will appear. You can see the furthest galaxies in Inner Space, you can see the moon, the stars and the invisible planets on the etheric, astral, mental, causal and Buddhic levels, but whatever you see, just stay focused on the act of meditation. At this stage you are calling down the Light, learning to *generate* the Light and understand how it works. Then, once you have the knowledge, you can channel that Light for all kinds of practical purposes.

As you develop Cosmic Vision you will understand that you are part of an indescribable, infinite living organism that has no beginning or end. In Inner Space, everything is connected because that is part of the unity of all things, so when you concentrate in the Third-Eye Centre you may have an experience in the Solar Plexus Centre, the Heart Centre or the Crown Centre. Acknowledge those experiences but stay focused in the Third-Eye Centre, which is the meditation you started doing. One of the rules of Meditation is to stick with what you started off with until you finish.

*****

You may also experience what we call *etheric matter*. As a child I perceived the etheric structure of the Universe as a wall of 'matter'. This is the etheric matter of Creation, the fundamental or primordial matter from which the atomic particles form regular matter. Science talks about dark matter and antimatter, but it is actually etheric matter, the original matter that we call the *Fifth Element* in Alchemy and which the Mystics have always known of. The Fifth Element is a homogeneous substance that pervades everything. It is the undifferentiated matter from which the atoms lose their own homogeneous vibration (or unified energy-field) and become objects, formulating themselves into "bubbles" that appear as human beings, animals, trees, plants, and so on. As physical forms, therefore, we humans are actually the Emptiness and the original matter is the real Fullness.

*****

The Gāyatrī Mantra *invokes* the Light, which either stays or disappears, so sometimes you need to repeat the Mantra and sometimes you don't. There is no need to repeat the Mantra once the Light has appeared; that would only disturb your vision. You have to find what works for you so that the Light remains and you don't disturb it. It's much like hunting, whose basic principle is not to frighten the prey, except in this case you're hunting for the Real, the True. But you must not frighten it because when you use your willpower, it is like frightening it and it will disappear. So if the Light appears, just observe it as it is, without trying to grab it and make it yours. In the First Gate, the Way of the Spiritual Warrior, the rule was: Surrender your ego to the Heart. *Surrender.* When you surrender, you drop your "I am" identity and the Other begins to be not afraid of you and comes closer and closer.

In Spiritual Life, if you do something aggressively it will come to nothing because the Inner Worlds accept passive rather than aggressive behaviour; it is just the way the internal structure of the Cosmos is. In the Old Testament, David wanted to run away from God and said, "If I go to the ocean you are there; if I go to the bottom of the sea you are there; if I go to the top of the mountains you are there; if I go to hell you are there" (PSALMS 139: 8). You cannot escape from Reality, but if you accept it, in that acceptance it will develop and grow.

*****

I'm telling you how to get to the Second Gate, but once the Gate opens, then you need to have guidance because you can be seeing all kinds of things—physical and etheric forces, astral forms and energies; entities that will take you to higher planes or drag you down to the lower worlds. Once your Cosmic Eye starts opening, you will encounter Reality in its vast form, which can be scary. In the Bhagavad-Gītā, Arjuna asked Kṛṣṇa to show him the real Universe, the real God, so Kṛṣṇa unveiled the Cosmos to him and Arjuna saw *everything*. The total Cosmic Vision, however, was so frightening that his consciousness couldn't handle it and he begged Kṛṣṇa to take it away.

As you experience Cosmic Vision you will come across the most amazing possibilities and things, and that's why you need a Teacher. There are lots of traps as well, because negative entities may appear. On the Astral and Mental Worlds beings can take any shape they want, so an elemental or subhuman being can tune into your mind, and if you have an image of, say, the Buddha or the Christ or Mohammed in your mind, it can assume that image. This is how mediums and channellers get tricked over and over again. When you start exploring the Inner Worlds you have to have real knowledge and guidance because everything you see is not what it appears to be—except of course when you've reached the Buddhic and Nirvāṇic dimensions, the upper regions where everything is as it is, where there is no possibility of deception.

THE WAY OF
TRANSCENDENTAL SOUND

Sound—the Basis of all Life

To understand the Science of Transcendental Hearing, whereby you learn to hear the Voice of God, we have to start with this fundamental understanding: the basic energy-reality of the Deity manifests itself in two forms—Sound and Light. In the beginning, before Creation, there was only total Silence, with no light or sound. We call this state the *Unmanifest Condition* and the first *pulsation* from that state came into existence as Sounding-Light. We refer to it as Sounding-Light because at first the Sound and Light are indistinguishable from each other, but as they come down through the various planes they become distinguishable. The Light aspect was described in the Second Gate, the Way of Cosmic Vision, and the Sound aspect is described in this Gate, the Way of Transcendental Sound.

The Way of Transcendental Sound starts with the Principle of Transcendental Hearing:

GOD'S VOICE IS EVERYWHERE.

"In the beginning was the Word and the Word was with God and the Word was God" (JOHN 1: 1). Many Christians read this in the Bible and then turn to the next page, thinking that they have understood the meaning of this statement. What the Christians call the *Word* is called Nāda or Śabda in Sanskrit and Logos in Greek. It is the Creative Sound, the Voice of God, the Creative Word that descends through the various planes of being and *creates* the planes. It created the Nirvāṇic World, the Kingdom of Light; the Buddhic World, the World of Unity and Oneness; the Mental World, which contains the Causal Worlds and the Heaven Worlds; the Astral World; and finally the Physical World. Sound is the way the Universe was made and the way the Universe is being maintained. Sound is the way *you* were made and the way you are being maintained. Sound is the basis of all Life; without it, nothing would exist.

The Creative Sound maintains the coherence of all things. If the Creative Sound, the Logos, withdrew from our Sun, the Sun would implode and leave nothing but empty space; if it withdrew from Earth, the planet would fizzle out and return to the original Primordial Substance; if it withdrew from you, you would die. In fact, it is the Inner Sound that keeps you alive on all levels: your astral body has its sound-structure and once that is withdrawn your astral body dissolves, and your mental body has its sound-structure and once that is withdrawn your mental body dissolves. Your Soul (your Causal Body) cannot be dissolved, however, because on that level the Word is pulsating eternally and without change, and therefore any beings who are in that energy-field cannot be changed or destroyed—they are *immortal*. It is only the personality that changes because in *this* world, the Word itself is always moving through the cycle of Creation-Maintenance-Dissolution.

So the Creative Sound, God's Voice, is everywhere: if you travel to the furthest galaxy you will still hear the same Voice of God and it can be distinguished as unique Sound-structures as it descends through the planes from the Causal World down. You can only hear these Sound-structures through your own inner being, but the Inner Ear is not functioning in the human being (in the same way as the Inner Eye is not functioning). So the Way of Transcendental Sound has techniques or processes that help you open the Inner Ear so that you can hear the melody of God's Voice inside you. Later you will hear the melody of God's Voice in the planet, in the stars and in the Cosmos. Inner Hearing increasingly expands in the same way as Inner Vision, so you may first hear a faint sound in your Inner Ear, but as you progress on the Way you will hear the hum of your whole aura and begin to sense that there are sounds outside your aura. Then you will hear the sounds of the internal structure of our planet, the sounds of the Astral World, the Causal Worlds, and so on until you hear the State of Unity, which is like a dynamic machine humming throughout all Creation.

Once you start practising the Way of Transcendental Sound and learn the art of listening inside, interestingly, you will learn to listen outside. In time you can develop Transcendental Hearing to such a degree that you hear sounds other people cannot. You can quite literally listen to the grass growing or hear what a dog is really saying beyond its bark. Everything in Nature can tell you its own state of being through sound. Sound is the power of creation, expression and dissolution *of* and *beyond* Nature. When Creation dissolves, the Sound will reverberate and return to a unified field of harmony and everything will dissolve back into the Unmanifest Condition.

This is all the understanding that is needed before you come on to the Way of Transcendental Sound. Each of these first three Gates can be practised by anybody and each one leads you from where you are at, your present human stage, to the stage where you become a Master of Wisdom or a Master of Love, in charge of not only your own destiny but also that of the planet. The personality life is not really that important; it is the destiny of the planet itself that is important.

Learning to Listen

To make the Third Gate understandable, we'll bring it down to the personality level so that you can relate it to your immediate life; otherwise, you may think it can only be practised by Buddhist monks or cloistered Christian clergy who contemplate all day and do nothing else. As your understanding develops you will realize that the Way of Transcendental Sound is actually transpersonal and limitless. On the personality level, however, in order to master the practical techniques of the Third Gate, you need to understand this key principle:

LEARN TO LISTEN. IN LISTENING COMES A NEW STATE OF AWARENESS, A TRANSFORMATION INTO A NEW STATE OF BEING.

For thousands of years, age after age, the Spiritual Hierarchy of Adepts has sent Avatāras and Teachers to explain exactly how the Universe is, to try to transform human consciousness, but very few people ever listened to them, and of those few even fewer understood them. Human ignorance has prevailed, and still does, for the simple reason that human beings don't listen; it is difficult to dispel Avidyā, Ignorance, on this planet.

So the first thing is to learn to listen. Of course, if you go to rock music concerts, you will notice two things: the music is loud and all the people there are listening. In other words, there are two aspects present: the music itself, which is just a form of sound, and the listening, which is the way to get to the sound. Some people like listening to classical music, which has the energy of Sattva—beauty, harmony and inspiration—and some people like to listen to pop music, which has the energy of Rajas, either in its positive form of overactivity or its negative form of destructiveness. On the physical level, therefore, there are basically two kinds of sound: that which destroys the principle of coherence in a person and that which uplifts and harmonizes a person. Sound is a powerful instrument in the physical world.

I'm bringing the science right down to the physical level because you have to do the same thing on the spiritual level, except that on the spiritual level you don't listen to classical music or pop music, you listen to another kind of sound—Transcendental Sound. But whether you listen outwardly to Sattvic or Rajasic sound or inwardly to Transcendental Sound, it all involves the act of *listening*. Remember, each Gate leads to Enlightenment, Eternal Life, and each Gate has its key to how you can attain Eternal Life. Listening is the key to the Third Gate.

Most of the time people think they listen but they don't listen at all; they just *interpret* what they hear according to what they want to hear. This is important because it is the source of international conflicts. A typical example was the League of Nations. It was formed after the First World War so that nations could talk together and prevent wars. They talked a lot but couldn't prevent the Second World War. Then the United Nations was formed for the same reason, but there are still wars everywhere now. Why? Because the representatives interpret what the other persons say according to their own understanding— nobody actually *listens*—so nothing ever really happens and there is no real peace on Earth.

What about the churches? The Pope calls for a big convocation of the Anglican Church, the Russian Orthodox Church and other churches. They discuss how all good Christians should unite and work together, everybody says their piece and they go home and do exactly the same as before. The big failure of human consciousness is that people interpret everything according to their preconceptions and their own belief system and background, and they never listen to what the other person is actually saying.

Humanity has lost the *art* of listening.

So we have to first learn to listen, which means being open to what the other person, group or religion is saying. Sometimes the other side may actually be right—and this realization will immediately change your level of awareness and you will see things from a different perspective. This does not necessarily mean that you accept everything, but the act of listening itself opens you up to see another way, or a hundred different ways, towards a solution. In other words, listening is a way of expanding awareness even on the physical level.

I'll give you an extreme example of not listening. Have you ever been approached by Jehovah's Witnesses or Mormons? It's impossible to communicate with them because they already have an answer, usually a quote from the Bible, even before you open your mouth. So it is impossible to say something to them from a broader perspective or tell them even a simple truth. It is a problem if people are so stuck in the workings of their mind that they are incapable of listening—and therefore incapable of bringing themselves to a new state of awareness. We call this *fundamentalism*. The fundamentalist state of mind thinks it knows everything; it is fixed and rigid. Fundamentalism in politics, society and religion is a primary cause of the endless conflict on this planet.

If you are truly able to listen to others without preconceptions, you can begin to see things in another light, which brings you to a new state of awareness, which produces a transformation within you—a transformation of your consciousness. On the spiritual level you cannot interpret or presume what God is saying according to what your religion has taught you. You either listen to what God is saying or you don't. You either hear the Truth or you don't. There is no interpretation of the Truth. When you can hear the Truth outwardly, then, as you do the inner practice, you will hear the Truth inwardly as it is unveiled to you.

PRACTICE

✳

For this Gate, the Way of Transcendental Sound, the practice you need to do is: *try to really listen to what other people say.* Truly listen, and then observe whether a new state of awareness arises within you. What is the new state of being and how did it change you? Practise listening in everyday life, because when you do the spiritual practices associated with this Gate, you will understand that God's Voice is everywhere, and this understanding will transform you into a new state of being.

The Sounds of Silence

If you are involved in the fields of medicine, psychology, psychiatry or any other healing profession, you may be familiar with the idea of some people being able to hear or see things that so-called normal people cannot hear or see. Traditionally, such people were considered to be insane and committed to a mental institution. Telling someone who has inner experiences that they are insane is doing them a great injustice, and it is usually due to lack of awareness in the medical profession. Most doctors believe that the physical body is the total human being and the physical world is the total reality, so they cannot treat people who experience something beyond the physical reality because they do not even believe in the possibility of such a thing.

Many so-called mental illnesses are not actually illnesses at all; they are simply cases of people perceiving things that others cannot perceive, such as visual or auditory sensations from the Astral World. Of course, when they try to explain these experiences to a psychiatrist, they are considered nutcases and sent to the hospital, where they are given drugs. The tragedy of medicinal drugs is that rather than healing people they actually reduce their sensitivity. That's because medicinal drugs are made from the Mineral Kingdom, which is three kingdoms *below* the Human Kingdom, far below the human level of awareness and intelligence. Drugs have their value, but modern society is overusing them to the point where we are densifying human consciousness and our physical bodies cannot register finer vibrations.

I will outline some of the inner experiences of Sound so that when you have these experiences you will understand that you are simply using a little more of the auditory faculty than the average person, that rather than being insane you are spiritually better off than those who cannot Hear.

I'll start with the Sounds of Silence, sounds you may already be able to hear in your present condition. You will likely recognize some of these sounds, and then rather than being afraid and going to the doctor, you will understand that what you are experiencing is not a sign of insanity but the miracle of Life, the activity of the Creative Power of God, the Creative Word, inside you. The very atoms of physical substance make sounds that are simply differentiations of the One Sound, the One Divine Creative Word—God in incarnation as It is expressing Itself.

At a later stage of this Path you will begin to hear how God is structuring matter on higher levels through the sounds of the Astral World and then the Causal Worlds, and so on. You will understand—through experience—how Divinity is actively creating and maintaining Creation, and you will understand it as the truth and reality of existence, not just as a philosophy. You will go through a vast range of experiences as you evolve on this Path from where you are now to the stage when you become the Master that you are on the Soul level.

Silence as such does not exist; it is simply that which we cannot hear. Because our physical hearing has such a limited range, what we do not hear appears as silence. Even when we experience the Astral World—in meditation or when we are out of the body at night—we only hear a certain range of sounds and the remainder of that vast spectrum of Sound registers as silence. As we progress up through the planes we can hear sounds that we know are the Life of the Deity, but what appears to be silence on each plane is simply that which we do not have the faculty to hear.

What you cannot see on all the Inner Planes appears as invisible and what you cannot hear appears as silence, but as you practise the techniques associated with the Second and Third Gates, you will develop your Seeing and Hearing faculties and you will begin to appreciate the amazing nature of Creation.

Ringing, Roaring, Buzzing, Hissing, Whistling, Clicking or Whooshing Sounds in Your Ears

These are some sounds you may already hear with (apparently) your physical ears. Many people experience a ringing in their ears or a roaring, buzzing, hissing, whistling, clicking or whooshing sound. These sounds are the activity of the Creative Word structuring the physical atoms of your body in a certain way to maintain your form and shape. Because of how the Creative Word interacts between the atomic structure of the physical body and that of the etheric-physical body, there is a certain sound-structure produced when the life-force hits the physical body structure, in the same way that a sound is produced when you pluck a stringed instrument or bang on a drum. The sound you hear is due to your Inner Ear opening a little, and you are hearing what is keeping you alive in Creation in this physical body.

Now, sometimes your sensitivity increases and you hear the sound more strongly or even continuously, twenty-four hours a day. Of course, it can be a nuisance when there is a buzzing in your ear and you want to go to sleep. If you are troubled by one of these sounds, what you should do is, rather than fighting it, listen to it and accept that it is there, like the air you breathe is there all the time. Go into the sound and locate the source of it—it could be in the etheric body, for example—and then the sound will disappear from your consciousness. If you try to fight it, it becomes worse because the energy of fighting it disturbs your whole equilibrium; instead, simply listen to it, accept it and focus on what you have to do. Then it will disappear and you will be able to sleep.

"Chin-Chin Chini-Chin" Sound

This is a sound you hear when your consciousness is moving out of the physical body and into the etheric body itself. There are many sounds you can hear as you move outside the physical body and begin to sense the astral and higher dimensions, but they are still within your own aura. In other words, it is not the Astral World you are hearing; it is how the Creative Word functions *inside* you in the deeper layers of your consciousness, how the Creator moves in the different regions from the physical to the etheric, astral, mental and causal regions. Accordingly, all the following sounds are also within your aura.

Bell, Conch Shell, Drums (Large and Small), Trumpet, Horn, Cymbals, Wind Instruments, Guitar, Vina, Violin, Harp, Harpsichord

This is the next layer of sounds you may hear inside. You have a whole orchestra inside you! And believe it or not, the musical instruments were invented from these sounds. They were first heard internally and then reproduced externally, so the physical part is only the externalization of the Inner Reality. You hear these sounds as your Inner Hearing becomes more sensitive and you move deeper within your own auric energy-field, into the regions of the astral body, the mental body and the causal body. Naturally, there are fewer people who can hear these sounds compared with those who hear the sounds connected to the etheric-physical part of the aura (ringing, roaring, buzzing). In the beginning stages, therefore, most people will first notice one of the more commonly heard sounds.

As a general rule, always listen to the strongest sound you can hear, and once you can identify with that sound, try to listen beyond it to another finer and subtler sound. Once you locate that sound, listen to it until it becomes strong and clear, then try to locate a yet finer sound, and so on. What you hear depends on which region of the astral or mental dimensions you can tune into. The first layer of etheric-physical sounds can be heard as unmelodious sounds, but you will hear the sounds of the Astral Plane and above as melodies, not complete works of music, of course, but as short, repeating melodies. This shows that the Creative Word produces a certain frequency or resonance inside you that sounds like part of a melodious song, which is why it is called the Heavenly Music or the Divine Orchestra within. At a much later stage when your Cosmic Hearing opens completely, you can hear the melodies simultaneously and it really does sound like a heavenly orchestra or symphony inside you.

Bird, Cricket, Cicada Sounds, Water Sounds—Waterfalls, Rivers, Lakes, Moving Water

The cricket or cicada sound is the Creative Word shaping the etheric substance, and the different types of bird sounds are the sounds of CIDĀKĀŚA, the Inner Space of the astral dimension. The water sounds are the astral substance in motion, and you can hear a variety of moving water sounds when you are tuned in to the astral energy of your aura.

Thunder, Lightning, the Roaring Ocean

These sounds can be heard when you start sensing your causal body in the deeper layers of Inner Space called the Causal World. There (within the inner dimensions of your aura) you can hear sounds like the rumbling of thunder or the roaring of the ocean, and sometimes you can even see flashes of lightning.

Silence (Buddhic World)

When you come to the Silence you are in the Buddhic World. You encounter the Silence *after* you have listened to all those other sounds, and it appears as silence because you have not yet awakened the Buddhic faculty of hearing. So you first have to awaken the Inner Hearing on the etheric, astral, mental and causal levels before the sounds of the Buddhic level can be heard. The Buddhic dimension is the World of Unity or Oneness, so when you have awakened the Inner Hearing faculty on that level you will experience what the Mystics have always spoken of: the Tao, Unity, Oneness, Bliss and Ecstasy.

On the practical level, these sounds can primarily be heard anywhere within your aura, but when you begin there may be a certain point of focus inside you that is easier to use. For instance, some people can hear sounds when they focus in the Heart Cakra. This is called ANĀHATA NĀDA, or the Inner Spiritual Sound. Some people can hear sounds in the left ear and some in the right ear; it is not the physical ear but rather that part of your inner mechanism or auric field. The last sounds—the thunder and roaring—and the Silence are experienced in the Causal Centre (above the head). The Buddhists call the Silence ŚŪNYA or ŚŪNYATĀ and the Ancients called it the *Emptiness*. Similarly, after reaching the Nirvāṇic World you will again perceive nothing. On that level this is called MAHĀŚŪNYATĀ (*Great Emptiness*). Again, with perseverance you will suddenly see the Bright Light and hear the omnific resonance of the Creative Word on that level.

To progress on the Way of Transcendental Sound you must be still. If you are not still, you cannot hear any sound. Every time you hear a sound, it makes your mind and inner being absolutely motionless, and in that motionless state you can hear the next sound, which leads to another motionless state and another sound, each time on a higher dimension until you come to the Thunder and Lightning inside you— and that will shake you up. When you first experience those sounds of the Causal World you may think that there is a wild storm going on outside and think you have to go out and bring in your washing! Then you realize that nothing is happening on the outside at all; it's all on the *inside*.

✻

There are spiritual techniques that are specifically Buddhist or Hindu or Christian, and a person has to be in the respective stream of energy to practise them, but the techniques we employ in the Nine Gates are not restricted to any race, colour, belief system, religion or political view. They can be practised by anybody who wants to attain Immortal Life—and that's where the beauty of this system is.

Meditation Technique 1: Intoning the "I" Sound

The first technique of the Way of Transcendental Sound is intoning the "I" sound in the Crown Cakra. This sound is not pronounced as in the English personal pronoun *I*, but as the *i* in "machine", that is, "ee".[11] This technique is the best one to start with for those who cannot hear internally, because it will open the Inner Ear.

First intone the "I" sound out loud to allow it to register in your mind, and then intone it silently with your attention focused in the Crown Cakra. The Crown Cakra is located slightly above the top of the head. Intoning the "I" sound there will stimulate your Inner Hearing faculty. Make a long, continuous "I" sound internally and then pause and start again. The main thing is to *listen* to the sound you are

---

[11] The problem with the English language is that the same letter can be pronounced in different ways, and the same sound can be written in many ways. Apart from the imperfections of the alphabetical system, the beauty of the English language is its extensiveness—its possibility of expansion is practically limitless—which makes it an amazing language to work with. The English language was chosen by the Spiritual Hierarchy as the medium for the communication of Esoteric Wisdom; no other language has as many esoteric books as English.

making. If your attention is sharp, the sound you are making will be sharp. If you are sleepy or hazy, then the sound becomes sleepy or hazy. You are creating your own sound, your own destiny, your own life. The brighter your sound, the brighter your life. If your consciousness is chaotic, it will be difficult for you to even make the sound at all. How sharp the sound is inside you indicates the consciousness and life stream inside you.

About This Technique

Keep in mind that when you make the "I" sound internally you should try to use as high a pitch as you can. Tibetan and Mongolian chanting uses a low, rumbling tone that comes from the Base Cakra, which is the ancient Atlantean system of chanting, an old form of working with magic. Intoning in that way takes us back to a very ancient consciousness, so we do not use it. The "I" sound should be a high pitch, and the higher the note, the better. You may start in a middle range because that is what your consciousness can hear, but try to refine it and gradually raise the pitch of the sound. The higher the pitch, the more easily it develops your Inner Hearing.

*****

Those who already have some Inner Hearing will hear ethereal sounds like crickets chirping or little bells tinkling. These sounds within your psychic mechanism are the ethereal part of the Word. So when you intone the "I" sound, you can also listen at the same time to those other sounds that are being made inside you and notice how your consciousness affects those sounds. By the way, the "I" sound is not the real sound of the Creative Word, but a sound you can relate to. The real Sound cannot be pronounced, so we have *imitation sounds*, like the vowels. They are imitation names of God as it were, ways that a human being can try to *imitate* the Logos.

*****

The "I" sound goes beyond the human range and becomes what could be referred to as *Devic* or angelic, and then it goes beyond that to the Archangelic Sound and then to the Logos, the very nature of God. In other words, what we hear is first a reflection of the Divine Word as it is trapped in Creation, trapped in the matter of our own system, and then the Divine Word trapped in the "matter" of the Inner Worlds. Then, beyond the Inner Worlds altogether, the Sound is *the* Word, *the* God.

It is like experiencing God in Its three forms—creative, preservative and destructive—*simultaneously*. This can also be observed in Nature. The whole cycle of life and death happens simultaneously in Nature, as it happens in the Divine Mind. At this moment galaxies are being created and galaxies are being destroyed; at this moment stars are being created and stars are being destroyed; at this moment some parts of Space are collapsing and some parts of Space are expanding. The scientific idea of the Big Bang assumes that all matter in Space was accumulated in one corner and then suddenly exploded in all directions. This is nonsense! Rather than being a haphazard event, Creation is an *engineered* reality, an eternal process of coming into existence, being and dissolution. It is an ongoing cyclic process until the end of Creation, when everything goes back to the Unmanifest Condition. Then, after several billion years, a time period called "Seven Eternities", the Cosmic Intelligence begins the whole process again.

*****

If you hear the Inner Sound when you are doing something mundane like washing dishes, it means that your attention is withdrawing to the inner dimensions, which is quite natural. Some people are so withdrawn that they could be called "spaced out", meaning that they are becoming more aware of the Inner Reality than the outer reality. Of course when that happens you have less desire to be active in this world. Some Indian Yogīs are so spaced out that they can't even feed themselves. They don't care what happens to the body, emotions or mind—which is immensely impractical when you live in the world.

So in our system we develop the "touch" of going within and then coming out and being busy doing things in Creation—like a swinging pendulum, in and out, in and out. Later there comes a stage where there is no swinging between the inner and the outer: you are inside and outside simultaneously. That is the condition of Cosmic Consciousness, where you are aware of what is happening in the Inner Worlds but are focused on the outer world because of what you are doing at the moment. Sometimes you focus on the Inner Worlds, but only when the time is right to do so. For instance, when your body is sleeping you can be superbly active on the inner dimensions because you do not have to worry about your body or the outer worldly conditions. Similarly, when you meditate you can withdraw and be busy in the Inner Worlds. The Law is that we are each here for a purpose and we must fulfil that purpose, while at the same time not neglect the Kingdom of God, our Inner Life.

That is the Way of the Nine Gates. And it is the Way of real Yoga, real Mysticism, real Sufism, real Buddhism, real Taoism, real Zen—*to be here and not be here at the same time.*

Meditation Technique 2: Listening to the Inner Sounds

In this meditation, you first sit still, calm yourself down and forget about all the mental chatter—the conversations and commentaries going on in your mind—and then bring your attention to a point of silence. It is only when you are reasonably still and quiet that you begin to hear Sound, and when you are really quiet you do not have to focus anywhere because the Sound is everywhere. The reason that people cannot hear the Inner Sound is because they are not quiet. The Sound is always there; all you need to do is develop Stillness.

With this technique there is no need to cross your legs or assume a Yoga posture or special sitting position because the Way of Seeing and the Way of Hearing have nothing to do with the physical body; they are *inner* faculties. So you can sit in any comfortable position—in an armchair or under a tree or even lying down—but be still and tune in internally. Once the mental noise has quietened down and you begin to hear the first sound, concentrate on that sound, without thinking about where it comes from or why it is there. Continue listening until you can pick up a more subtle sound and then focus on that. Continue to do that until your consciousness moves beyond your auric field and then do the same thing in the interdimensional Space, thereby tuning into the various stages of Sound.

About This Technique

The key to the Way of Transcendental Sound is not actually sound but *silence*. You can only hear to the extent that you are silent; the more noisy you are inside, the less you hear. This is part of the esoteric understanding of the Spiritual Path. The idea of silence is important no matter which Path you follow, and it is especially important in this one.

*****

Listening to the Inner Sounds can be practised as a formal meditation, but in the Way of Transcendental Sound (as in the Way of Cosmic Vision and to a certain point the Way of the Spiritual Warrior) a meditation can also be spontaneous. So the process of listening can be started while walking on a beach or through a forest or while gazing at the stars; it can begin in a spontaneous manner anywhere, if you are in the mood and you manage to generate silence inside. Sometimes you can be watching a butterfly or looking at a flower, and once your mind has quietened down you can hear the Sound, depending on how far you have progressed with your Inner Hearing meditation. The process automatically starts once you are quiet and still inside, so it doesn't always have to be a formal meditation session.

*****

If you hear one of the causal sounds, the thunder or the ocean roar, you may feel as if you were hit by lightning and your whole body may shake. It simply means that at that time your mind is not involved and your consciousness is simply registering the full velocity of the Etheric Current. Sometimes, between sleeping and waking, when your consciousness is not in the physical body but not quite in the astral body, you can feel a strong pulsation throughout your whole body because you have managed to identify with the Creative Word as it is pulsating in the etheric dimensions. When you fully identify with the sound it can be quite a shattering experience because of its intensity and power, but there is a safety mechanism that prevents you from fully identifying with the sound.

*****

Sitting by the ocean or sitting under a tree can be helpful. Some trees don't like human beings (which is understandable), but some trees will allow you to sit under them and actually help you to attain Inner Transformation. You may feel such a tree harmonizing your spinal system, your whole inner being, helping you get to Samādhi (Causal Consciousness, or Mystical Consciousness) quickly.

*****

As you progress beyond the preliminary stages of the Way of Cosmic Vision, the Way of the Transcendental Sound or even the Way of the Spiritual Warrior, you realize that what you experience is limited in that moment by the human physical body. Once you move beyond it into the etheric-physical body or the astral body, your sensation of seeing, hearing and touching increases a thousandfold. In your etheric-physical body you can sense the etheric energies of the trees and plants and all of Creation flowing in and around you, and furthermore you are aware of these energies through any part of your body. In your astral body you are aware of the elementals, angels and a myriad of beings, and the further you move up the planes, the greater your sensitivity becomes. Then you will begin to understand the vastness of the Cosmic Reality and you will realize how tremendously amazing the Creative Word is—that it is God *in* Incarnation.

THE WAY OF
THE DIVINE BREATH

The Universal Life-Force

The Way of the Divine Breath is a most amazing path because you are practising it all the time! You have been practising it since the moment you were born—but unconsciously, because you were never told about it. If you had been instructed about the Divine Breath, you would be already walking in the clouds with the Buddhas.

I will start by explaining some words which may help you realize what you have been missing out on all your life.

TAI CHI. *The Great Power*
PRĀṆA. *The Life-Force*
SHEKINAH. *The Divine Emanation*
PNEUMA. *The Spirit*
SPIRITUS SANCTUS. *The Holy Breath*
RUACH ELOHĪM. *The Breath of the Gods, the Creative Hierarchies*
ŚAKTI. *The Divine Energy*

Would you believe that all these words refer to the same thing? All this time, you have been working with *the Great Power, the Life-Force, the Divine Emanation, the Spirit*, and nobody told you.

This background is important so that you understand that the Way of the Divine Breath is about more than just breathing in and out, that it is part of a much larger reality.

THE UNIVERSAL LIFE-FORCE SUSTAINS ALL BEINGS GREAT AND SMALL, HUMAN AND ANGELIC, SOLAR SYSTEMIC AND ATOMIC.

There is a field of energy around our Mother Earth in which every creature breathes in and breathes out. The human beings, animals, plants, elementals, angels and archangels—all the many diverse visible and invisible beings on the planet are breathing in and out that same force. You may call it by any one of the aforementioned names or you may call it the *Universal Life-Force*, or one simple word: *Life*.

I find it amusing when I read about scientists who say there *could* be "life" somewhere else in the Universe, that some kind of microscopic organism or structure with a similar composition to ours could have evolved on some distant planet, but they can't be sure because it is too far away to measure. And this is from the exalted realms of the scientific world! This is the scientific idea of life! Life is here and everywhere, permeating every planet and every dimension. Nothing can exist without it. Life existed long before science, long before Humanity; it is the essential thing on which the whole of Creation moves. All of the above names of the Universal Life-Force together mean "Life".

Now, you can sense the massive field of energy around our Mother Earth when you go to places like the Himalayan Mountains or the deserts of Mongolia, where the planet still retains its own natural energy-field and you can feel the high-frequency energy of the atmosphere. That is *Her* life-force, the energy that keeps our Mother Earth alive, the energy that She receives from the Sun, the Solar Logos.

Every planet receives energy from the Solar Logos ("our Father in Heaven"), who continually sends out a tremendous radiant energy-field that bombards all the planetary systems and interplanetary space to the boundary of the Solar System, on all the Seven Planes of Reality. The Solar Logos radiates out this massive force continually from the time He is born to the time He dies, giving it to the lower entities—the Planetary Logoi and, within the Planetary Logoi, the many hierarchies that exist on the visible and invisible dimensions. This is called the *Great Sacrifice*.

As this great Cosmic Being pours out His life-force *as a service*, He is evolving because He is receiving compensation for it: He receives a movement of *Karma* whereby He is bombarded by the higher-frequency energy of a Super-Sun that pours *His* life-force into the Solar Logos. Our Solar System is one of twelve Solar Systems that are the twelve Cakras of a Super-Sun that gives cosmic energy to the twelve Solar Logoi. This circulation of Life continues in an ever-increasing way from the minute to the vast, in accordance with the Cosmic Law of Service: if you do something for others you get back a higher-frequency energy in return.

The *Life-Force* (and all its alternative words) is simply the Solar Logos giving His life out. The planets absorb that life and transmute it for their own living processes, and the living beings within the planetary structures take *their* portion of that life for their survival. This is how the system works, and when you first started breathing you began the tremendous process of receiving and giving out the Universal Life-Force. So if you understand that you have been doing a "cosmic work" since birth, then you can really start doing the Cosmic Work.

Incidentally, the Life-Force is well illustrated in the *Star Wars* movies. The main idea of the Star Wars movies is that there exists an all-embracing Universal Life-Force throughout the Galaxy (which is one hundred percent true), and within those galactic systems there are 'goodies' and 'baddies' (also perfectly true). Of course, the baddies (the "Dark Side") use that force for selfish ends, while the goodies understand this principle of the Universal Life-Force and try to develop it inside themselves to become Jedis, or Knights of the Life-Force. In other words, the main theme of the movies is to become aware of the Life-Force and consciously use it for the benefit and upliftment of others.

The point of this is to put everything into context for you so that when you work with the exercises in the first stage of the Way of the Divine Breath, you will realize that you are doing much more than making yourself fitter and healthier: you are working with Mother Earth, using Her life-force and energy to transmute *your* life-force and energy, expand your inner awareness and get in touch with the planetary life-force. You will learn how to manipulate your breath and slowly become aware that it is part of the planetary breath cycle. Later on you will realize that the planetary life-force is part of the solar systemic life-force, and when you become a Master you will realize that even the solar systemic life-force is just a fragment of the Universal Life-Force, the infinite, absolute, boundless energy source from which every star system and galaxy live.

The Life-Force and You

Remember, the Way of the Spiritual Warrior (Surrender), the Way of Cosmic Vision (Seeing), the Way of Transcendental Sound (Hearing) and the Way of the Divine Breath (Breathing) are all *gateways to immortality*. They were designed to create the conscious experience of immortality, whereby you realize your oneness with the indestructible *power* that always was, is and will be. That power can change, because power transforms itself, but it can never be destroyed. Scientists *re*discovered that which was taught by the Ancients, that energy can be transformed but not destroyed. This great power, by whatever name it is called, is the source of all systemic and evolutionary creation processes, so once you are hooked onto that vast energy-field you automatically become immortal, eternal, in a deathless condition.

The Way of the Divine Breath is about recognizing what your breath is on a deeper layer inside you, then moving outside your own auric energy-field to sense the planetary breath and then the solar systemic breath and so on. This is a simple and natural process. Nothing needs to be imposed from the outside because you have the faculties you need within you already. In fact, human beings have always possessed these faculties, *because* there is a larger reality. These faculties are simply imitating that larger reality in our personal existence: we see, we hear and we surrender, as the planet does to the Solar System, as the Sun does to the Super-Sun, as the Super-Sun does to the Lord of the Galaxy, as the Lord of the Galaxy does to Parabrahman, the Absolute Reality. These processes have always existed, and once you discover that, you liberate yourself from identification with human limitation, from the idea that you are a miserable, worthless human being.

You may think you are a failure and feel that the end of your life has arrived. But what if you start sensing that you are part of a great reality, a great life-force? When you are on that larger wave, everything that human beings strive to attain seems so small, too insignificant to have a breakdown about. This is where the problem with the education system lies, where the wrong ideas of life are taught—that success in life means becoming a lawyer, dentist or accountant and earning lots of money. So you work to achieve that and then realize that you are not happy at all. I am not saying that you shouldn't go to school or work. I am saying that it is not your cosmic goal; it is not what being human is about. Whatever we do on this physical plane is part of the simple necessities of life, and there is nothing wrong with that, but you have to see where it fits into the larger, cosmic picture.

People feel they have to do what society expects them to do and then go into terrible states of depression if they think they have failed. But they have not failed; it is just their vision that is too narrow. What if they said, "Wow, I am breathing in the great Life-Force, I am seeing the Eternal Light, I am One with the Divine"? Where is the failure? You can fail a human objective but you cannot fail Life itself because you *are* Life, you are part of the Universal Life-Force. You cannot fail that.

This is why it is so important to educate Humanity regarding the *true* vision and purpose of life. Once you start experiencing the greater Life through the Way of the Spiritual Warrior, the Way of Cosmic Vision, the Way of Transcendental Sound or the Way of the Divine Breath, you will be forever happy because you know that you cannot fail. These Ways teach you how to live the Cosmic Life. When you sincerely practise and truly understand any one of them, you will begin to live as a citizen of the Cosmos, rather than a citizen of a tiny community with limited ideas. You will have a different understanding and a different attitude to life because you realize that you are part of a much larger reality. Then, you will be bubbling inside with the joy that comes from never losing your inner connectedness with the greater Reality.

Remember, this does not mean that you should give up your job and responsibilities. If there is something you have to do, you do it. This is the Way of the Warrior. The Warrior always fights for what is right, for the Light, for the unveiling of Reality for the greater community and all Humankind. For the last three thousand years in India, this idea was wrongly interpreted: everything was regarded as Māyā (illusion, limitation) and so why bother with everyday life? This is a wrong understanding and India degenerated because of it; for this world is not an illusion but part of the Ultimate Reality. It is simply that this world has certain laws and is structured in certain ways (just as the Astral World or Nɪʀᴠāṇᴀ has its own laws and ways of doing things), but in its own category it is real. Every part of the Cosmos is structured and purposefully directed and you have to discover the functional laws of each plane and comply with them, and try to do things in the best way.

There is a scene in *Star Wars* where one of the surviving Jedis kills someone for no reason other than anger. The interesting part is that Yoda (the Master Warrior with Cosmic Consciousness) was able to feel this Jedi committing a wrong act even though he was on another planet. You might think this is just a silly Hollywood idea, but it isn't. At a certain level of spiritual evolution you can be so in tune with the whole Solar System (and beyond) that you can actually feel a change in the radiation of the Universal Energy-Field when something wrong is happening. This is what happens when you are working with the Life-

Force, the Divine Breath. Of course, if you have opened your Inner Eye, then you can see exactly where it is happening; if you have opened your Inner Ear, you can actually hear the cries of those in distress; and if you are a Spiritual Warrior standing in the Light, you immediately know that something is wrong in the alignment of the Light.

The One Life-Force

With each of the Gates discussed thus far, we have outlined certain keywords you should live by, apart from formal meditation techniques. That's because it's not enough just to do a technique or meditation; your way of life has to change. So we have to give you understanding, what you need to restructure your whole existence. The Way of the Divine Breath, therefore, has two parts: learning how to breathe and what breathing does to you, and acquiring an understanding of life itself, which starts with this simple truth:

IT IS THE SAME LIFE-FORCE, ONLY USED DIFFERENTLY BY DIFFERENT INTELLIGENCES.

This is something you can put into practice by observing your surroundings. Look at a little bug and watch what it does with its feelers, and then think: "It's the same life-force as in me, only it is used differently by a different intelligence." A tree uses the same life-force, an animal uses the same life-force, an elemental and an angel use the same life-force, the minutest atom and the largest galaxy use the same life-force. There's only one Life-Force, one Divine Breath—but used differently by different intelligences.

In other words, there are two things in the Cosmos: Intelligence and Life-Force. The atoms are intelligent in their own dimensional reality; they act according to their intelligence, arranging themselves into cells in your body or in a plant or animal, and those cells are also intelligent, according to their level of evolutionary attainment. A mineral, a stone, has its own intelligence according to the level of evolution of the Mineral Kingdom. Each creature—animal, human, angel— has its own level of intelligence.

Make it your way of life to observe that whatever you come across has an intelligence level and it can function according to its intelligence, and then identify that it is using the same life-force as you use. Once you start observing people and realizing that they are using the same life-force according to their level of intelligence, you will stop being judgemental and critical of others. Don't compare yourself to others; that's not the idea. The idea is to observe that the same Force, the same Life, the same Reality works in everything, but there are different levels of Cosmic Evolution or Intelligence at work. But do not concentrate on the intelligence part of it but on the fact that everything uses the same life-force—the same fundamental Life which we call the Divine Breath, Tao, Tai Chi, Śakti or Shekinah. It is this realization that makes you one with other people, one with your circumstances, one with Reality.

Most people don't understand that a spiritual life is a practical life where your whole life is being transformed. It's not just about practising a meditation technique and then watching a TV programme. That's not enough of a transformation. Each of these Paths requires that you live life in a transformative way. Doing spiritual exercises on a regular basis is a total necessity, yes, but it is not enough to put you on the Way of Enlightenment. Do you think Spiritual Masters just sit around and meditate all day? No. They live life but in a different way. They perceive things in a different way.

So the more you are able to tune into the Life-Force, the more you realize how unbelievable Reality is. And then you will understand that Life is actually impossible to describe or comprehend in its totality, that it is the most beautiful thing you can be a part of.

The Life-Force is vast and billions of creatures are breathing it in and breathing it out. *You* are part of the great circulation of the Life-Force, and your life and health depend on it.

HEALTHY BODY, HEALTHY MIND, HEALTHY EMOTIONS HAVE TO DO WITH THE CORRECT CIRCULATION OF THE LIFE-BREATH IN YOUR AURIC BEING (PERSONALITY).

By *auric being* we mean the totality of your energy-field, your total personality, what you are in your physical, etheric, astral, mental and causal bodies.

Once the healing profession starts working from this understanding, things will change in every aspect in all the medical fields. How many doctors think about the correct circulation of the life-breath? None. Yet all your physical, emotional or mental problems are due to the incorrect circulation of the life-breath inside you; the life-force inside you is not functioning as it was originally intended by the Divine Mind. That's because, when the life-breath is circulating correctly, a person's actions, emotions and thoughts are all correct. The only way to understand this is to have a larger view of existence.

As a human being, you have your own life-breath, which comes in from the planetary energy-field (not the scientific energy-field, but the *real energy-field*, which includes the invisible forces by which our Planetary Mother breathes in and out the Cosmic Life). All human beings breathe in and breathe out, and in the process they use and transform the planetary life-force and then give it back to Mother Earth. Therefore, human beings cannot be healthy while there are millions of unhealthy people utilizing the planetary energy in a negative way. Human beings cannot be healthy while we are exterminating the forests and the animal life on a large scale. In other words, human beings cannot be healthy while we are causing a vast unbalance in the energy-field of Nature, *because all things are interdependent.* There's only one Life-Force permeating all of Creation.

The energy-field of the planet is poisoned and degenerated and some parts of the planet are worse than others. Some countries are totally disorganized, chaotic and negative, but because their inhabitants are breathing in and out the life-force, they are projecting the same chaotic, negative energy onto the planetary energy-field and spreading it to other countries as well. This is something we really have to understand. We are creating or destroying the planetary life-force, contributing either positively or negatively, by the way we think and the way we do things. There is no in-between; we either give a positive or a negative value to life.

People talk about poisoning the atmosphere with car fumes and factory fumes, which is physical poisoning, but nobody thinks of the psychological and emotional poisoning of the life-force itself. So the question is: Can we be healthy when the planetary energy-field we live in is poisoned? In the olden days, people understood the way of Nature a bit more. In nineteenth-century novels you read about doctors telling their patients they need a change of location, that they should go to the sea or the countryside for a few months. They realized that maybe the energy-field of the place where the person lived wasn't right, that it was not bright enough, that there was not enough Prāṇa, or life-force, in the air. This recognizes that some parts of the planetary energy-field are purer than others, places where Mother Earth can breathe more naturally, and that some parts are so impure that it's almost impossible to be healthy in that environment.

A number of years ago there was a series of murders in England committed by young people, even children as young as eight years old. The social workers, psychologists and politicians began to wonder what was wrong with society, why there were suddenly all these murders by young people. But if you go to the places where the murders happened, and if you are sensitive and can feel the energy of those places, you will notice that they are grimy and depressive. If children are born into such a negative environment, they will automatically absorb the violent energy of that place and unconsciously start imitating it and living it at quite an early age. It doesn't make any difference how many rules governments make; what is important is the place people live in. You cannot have a healthy environment where millions of people are producing negative energies through their actions, emotions and thoughts.

The Physical Body Is Not Independent

The problem with the medical field is that most people in the healing professions always try to fix the physical body, believing that it's some sort of an independent organism with no connection to anything or anybody else. As long as they think like that, health will always be a problem and keeping society in a good state of health will be impossible.

The way you work on the physical, emotional and mind levels is all part of your total energy-field, your auric being. So when something is not functioning, of course, you have the symptoms of physical, emotional or mental ill health. This is where modern healers fail because they look at symptoms, thinking that they are the cause. But they are not the cause; they are the end product. The cause is an imbalance somewhere in the person, including their physical breathing and their attitudes, thoughts, feelings and actions. When all these things are put into harmony, the symptoms disappear. In the future, when Mankind is not so materialistic and a little more enlightened, doctors and healers will look at your whole life and not just where you are sore, and rather than concentrating on pills, which are a temporary solution, they will teach people how to *breathe life* correctly. Giving people pills is easy but it doesn't stop them from wrong thinking, wrong feeling and wrong action.

It is a matter of understanding that whatever you do impacts on a larger part of reality than just your immediate environment, just like an oil spill in the ocean kills the fish in that area and then washes up on the shore and affects the birds that live on the shoreline. This is why we have to look at the whole of human society and the planet itself as one reality. When there are millions of human beings doing wrong things, our Mother Earth has to panic because Her life-breath is being destroyed. As we mentioned before, She is dependent on the Cosmic Breath and gets the Life-Force from our Sun for Her own life process, but we have managed to poison Her breath, the energy She gets from the Sun, through all the massive nonsense we do.

Everything is interconnected and is dependent on the one Life-Force. That is the reality. So what are we going to do on a practical level?

Firstly, you have to realize your own interdependence, that you are breathing the one Life that every other creature breathes in and out, and that you *do* have a responsibility with what you do with your breath, which includes your whole life stream—your thoughts, feelings and physical efforts. Therefore, you must make sure that the energy emanating from you impacts others and the environment in a positive, healthy way.

This requires that you look at life in a much broader way, including the way you relate to others. Opinions are real. Emotions are real. Actions are real. They are all energy particles inside your auric energy-field and they are sent out into your environment, to other people, to animals and plants and to the invisible dimensions. If you send out a negative wave your experience of life becomes negative; you will have accidents and bad things happening to you. If you are full of brightness inside, things will work out for you and you will be directed to something that helps you move to the next step of your spiritual development. What you send out you get back; it is just how Life is.

So try to be more positive and brighter in what you are doing and in the way you look at others, because we are either helping our planet suffer, or helping our planet become healed.

Sō-Hang Natural Breath Meditation

The Sō-Hang Natural Breath Meditation[12] is the easiest way to approach the Divine Breath. The purpose of this technique is, firstly, to make you realize that you are a living being because your breath is life, and secondly, to help you understand how your breath is connected to the greater breath of the Earth, the Universal Energy-Field around and within everybody and all of Nature.

There are several variations of this technique but this is the simplest and easiest: Concentrate on the tip of your nose or in the Third-Eye Centre and breathe in and out. As you breathe in, mentally say "Sō", and as you breathe out, mentally say "Hang".

(Breathe in) "Sō"… (Breathe out) "Hang"…

(Breathe in) "Sō"… (Breathe out) "Hang"….

Completely relax and simply allow the breath to come in, and when it feels like it needs to go out, let it go out. It doesn't matter which breath is short or which is long or how long the pause between breaths is. Simply follow what is natural for you at the time.

---

[12] For the correct pronunciation of this Mantra, see the Sanskrit Pronunciation Guide at the end of the book.

About This Technique

Some breathing techniques involve counting as you breathe in, hold your breath and then breathe out. The problem, however, is that your attention is divided because it is largely on the act of counting, which involves the mind. It is a completely wrong method. Another wrong technique involves using a rosary and flicking a rosary bead each time you say a mantra, because, again, most of your attention goes into your hand moving through the beads and not to the mantra. In this meditation, you keep your attention on the breath itself.

*****

The first practical application of this technique is that it calms your mind. This can be useful after an argument, or before an argument (which is even better because there will be no argument). So when you feel the need to be calm, sit down and do this breathing technique. Allow Mother Nature to breathe in and out of you and then you will begin to feel harmonized. So that is the first application on the *physical* level.

The second, and deeper, application is that during meditation it will gradually lead you to the state referred to in Yoga literature as YOGA-NIDRĀ, the "sleep of the Yogī". Yoga-Nidrā does not mean that you actually go to sleep but you have the sensation of going to sleep. It is like you are crossing a bridge from your consciousness *here* to a consciousness *there*. Between those two states of consciousness there is a blank, sleepy state: Yoga-Nidrā.

This means that during meditation you may suddenly lose your waking consciousness but you know that you have been 'somewhere' when you return to waking consciousness. This may happen many times, but if you persevere with the Sō-Hang Breath Meditation, it will take you through the stage of Yoga-Nidrā to the *Awakening* inside.

You will suddenly awaken in that other dimension and be completely awake in that other reality. In other words, your consciousness will be able to function in another dimensional level and you will be awake on the inside, not just on the outside.

There are even deeper applications, of course, but we have to start with what can be applied on the physical level in the here and now, and this technique can radically change your life on the physical dimension straight away. Within two or three weeks of doing this you will be a different person. As you persevere, there will come the inner effects whereby you begin to sense the inner side of things, which will lead to even more amazing experiences.

*****

We are all absolutely unique individuals, the Life-Force within us is slightly different, and that gives a different colouration to the way we experience things. People will have different experiences of the same meditation practice, depending on their state of consciousness at the time, their particular situation, their readiness and many other factors. The experiences will be different, but the ultimate results will be the same.

*****

Natural breathing is the quickest way to realize that you are breathing the energy of Mother Earth, transforming it through your own system and giving it back to Mother Earth. Of course, you don't think of these technicalities; you don't think, I'm breathing in Mother Earth and I'm breathing out Mother Earth. In other words, there is no mental activity. Just breathe in and breathe out without trying to regulate your breathing with your mind.

It is interesting that when women are together, because of the nature of the receptive Feminine Mind, they often think together or breathe together. Because their breath is more attuned to the Universal Energy-Field, they can commune or communicate in a more simple and natural way that does not involve the intellect. In contrast, the male wants to communicate through the intellect. With this natural breath technique you will be able to sense your connectedness to other people, not as a mental idea but as a practical reality. Through the breath you will be aware of a natural and spontaneous connection to a person, cat, dog, flower or whatever.

*****

Keep it simple and let Nature do the work. Nature will reform you by Herself, because once you are on this Path you will be guided by the Invisible Nature—the Devas, elemental beings and angelic beings working on the etheric-physical dimensions. Once you consciously turn your attention inside for the purpose of achieving Immortality, they will see what you are doing and help clear the way for you from within the inner dimensions. If you have a selfish purpose for what you are doing, if you want to become a fantastic magician and command everybody and everything, there will be no help for you from the Inner World. In this way, the Inner World is like a mother, which is why we call it Mother Nature; She really will look after you like a mother.

*****

Like all the techniques in the Nine Gates, this one will lead you beyond the Astral World, the Mental World and the Causal World to the Buddhic Plane. As already mentioned, there comes a problem at a certain point when you do not have the faculty to embrace the Buddhic World and have to develop that faculty, which is called the *Buddhic Vehicle*, or in Theosophical language, the *Buddhic Body of Light*. This body enables us to sense the entire Buddhic dimension and embrace the profound Love-Wisdom Energy of that dimension. This faculty will develop through the practice of meditation techniques like this one and through the *will* of the Soul inside you, because the Buddhic Body of Light is developed in two directions: from the personality level, as you continue your spiritual practice, and from the Soul level, as the Soul works downward to unify its own field of awareness with that of the personality. It is a conjoint work of you as the Soul and you as the personality, and when the two unite, that Light Body suddenly starts to function and through it you can experience the Buddhic World. Then you will have what we call *the Great Awakening*.

A problem with the Spiritual Path is that if you do not work at it on the personality level, you will never achieve these results. You either have to work at it in this lifetime or have worked at it in previous lifetimes—like Krishnamurti, Ramana Mahārṣi and other Sages. Some people are born with this Body of Light already formed and only need to learn to reconnect to it in this lifetime, and so it is easier and quicker for them.

The Equalizing-Breath Meditation

In the martial art schools they do certain breathing techniques to change the length of the life-breath. In Yoga schools they breathe to bring more harmony into the internal energy stream. This technique is called the Equalizing Breath because it makes the incoming life-force equal to the outgoing life-force. It harmonizes your in-breathing and out-breathing, the energy you receive with the energy you give out, so that once you learn to do that you will be able to harmonize with other people.

To do this technique, first focus your attention at the tip of your nose. We focus at the tip of the nose because there is a small cakra there, in the auric energy-field, and when activated it becomes a powerful centre that helps awaken the Third Eye. That is why Yoga books often instruct the reader to focus at the tip of the nose. It has nothing to do with the nose itself but with the activation of that minor cakra.

Before you start, realize that your life is part of the Divine Life. Then, with your attention focused at the tip of the nose, breathe in and out, feeling how that energy comes in and goes out of you. We circulate the life-force all the time. Being aware of this circulation in and out will help you understand how the planetary energy-field is always circulating in and out, and gradually you will sense how energy is circulated between people. It is a way of opening yourself up to working in a larger and more comprehensive way. Be as simple as possible. Focus at the tip of your nose, breathe and see what happens.

About This Technique

You may have noticed that when you do different activities, the life-force, the life-breath, changes inside you. Have you noticed that when you go to the seashore and there is a fresh breeze blowing, you breathe deeper? Or when the air is still or the energy of your immediate environment is unmoving, then you feel sleepy? Have you noticed how you breathe when you are angry? Some people can get so angry that they actually stop breathing, stop receiving the life-force. Our life-force adapts itself to our feelings, thoughts and activities. Once you realize that your mechanism for breathing in the energy of life is adapting to you, then you can reverse the process and work directly on the life-force in order to change your breathing mechanism and change your interconnectedness and your energy level.

If you practise the Equalizing-Breath Meditation for a few weeks, your inner psychic mechanism, your auric energy-field, will begin to operate in a rhythmic, harmonious way and to set up a steady, peaceful rhythm, breathing in and breathing out. When that happens then naturally your mind and emotional body will be in a state of Sattva. People crave harmony, so they will notice that you are a happy person who is easy to talk to. You will feel more balanced and your whole attitude to situations and events will completely change. Instead of reacting angrily, violently or miserably to something, your reaction will be even and you will be able to deal with the situation more easily. Even the most terrible news won't stop you from breathing normally and getting the full energy stream from the atmosphere.

You can't deal with a situation if you are breathing disharmoniously because you can only react according to how you breathe; that is, your physical action follows your internal psychic stream. If your internal psychic energy stream is harmonious and positive, then your physical response to the situation will also be positive and you will be able to deal with it. If your internal psychic energy stream is disjointed then your actions will be disjointed. It's quite simple.

*****

If you feel pain in any cakra during meditation, it means that the life-force is trying to move there but it cannot flow through because the way is blocked. (Energy is like water and it can either flow through something or be contained, like water flows through a sieve or is contained in a pot). The reason for such blockages is the wrong actions and thoughts of the human family. Nowadays there is a lot of awareness around mothers not smoking or drinking during pregnancy because it can harm the baby, which is perfectly true, but there is no awareness of the damage that a mother can do to her baby through wrong (negative) thoughts and emotions. The negative energy is transferred to the baby and consequently the baby is born with a cakra system that is already blocked. People are born with crippled energy systems and spend the rest of their lives wondering why they are not healthy.

Harmonizing your life and breathing in and out in a larger way and with a greater understanding will dissolve those negative energies and unblock your internal energy system. When the energy is flowing correctly inside you, you breathe deeply with your whole physical body, astral body, mental body and your living Soul. In other words, you breathe Life in and out, not just through your nose but through your whole being.

*****

There are three major ways of spiritual experience: seeing, hearing or touching (not the physical touch but the inner touch through the psychic mechanism). Depending on their nature, some people are visual, some are auditory and some are better with inner touch. Everyone is born with one of these possibilities, or combinations in different proportions of each, and if you practise the faculties you don't have, you will slowly learn to see, hear or touch and evolve on all these particular paths.

*****

The minor cakra at the tip of the nose is the gate to the space-time-continuum. When it opens, you will understand what Space and Time really are, and you will realize that they don't exist. In Nature there is no Time and there is no Space. A flower exists and grows as a flower, without any concept of time or spatial awareness. Space and Time are concepts invented by humans so that we can have an organized structure of life here, and you will realize that when the cakra opens.

THE FIFTH GATE

THE WAY OF
DIVINE SOUND

The Way of Divine Sound is not the same as the Third Gate, the Way of Transcendental Sound, which deals with Nāda, the Inaudible Sound. That is the *passive* path of Sound, whereas the Way of Divine Sound is the *active* path of Sound. You will see that there is a huge difference between the two.

The Fifth Gate, the Way of Divine Sound, consists of three practices:

a) Mantra Repetition

b) Chanting

c) Devotional Acts and Rituals Using Mantric Sounds

The latter does not refer to all acts of devotional service but to rituals or acts *that use mantric sounds*. For example, the following practices use mantric sound and are part of this Way: the Roman Catholic Mass when it was sung in Latin; rituals of the Greek Orthodox Church sung in Greek; and Coptic Mass rituals sung in the original ancient Coptic language. If a ritual contains specific mantric sounds, whether Buddhist, Christian, Hindu or whatever, then it comes under the Way of Divine Sound.

Many of you have been practising this Way because it is widely used in all religions everywhere, but of course the religions do not understand what is behind it. So I will try to explain to you the esoteric side of this Path, which is a science with a particular background, knowledge and practice. The simplest way to define this science is with the Sanskrit term Mantra-Śakti, meaning the "Power of Mantra" or the "Mantric Energy".

MANTRA-ŚAKTI IS THE CREATIVE WORD UTTERED BY INTELLIGENT BEINGS TO BRING FORTH A MANIFESTATION OR TO TRANSFORM EXISTING CONDITIONS BY CONSCIOUS VIBRATION.

Already you may be starting to realize that this science is much larger than what you previously understood. In fact, all of the Nine Paths are cosmic but they have to be brought down to the level of the personality to start with so that you understand how they relate to *you*. Otherwise, a cosmic principle remains only a philosophy, and then you say, "So what!"

So, *Mantra-Śakti is the Creative Word uttered by intelligent beings.* Who are the *intelligent beings* we refer to? We refer here to some human beings, some angelic beings, some of the great cosmic Gods and Goddesses (called the ELOHĪM in Hebrew), some of the great Devas (which means the "Shining Ones" in Sanskrit) and other beings you have not heard of. There are twelve intelligent Creative Hierarchies in our Solar System and every one of them uses Mantra-Śakti to bring forth a new manifestation or change an existing condition by *conscious Vibration*, in other words, by using Mantra.

This means that when you chant, when you practise mantra repetition or a ritual that involves a mantra, you are actually doing the same thing as millions of conscious, intelligent beings in the Cosmos: using the Creative Word, the Logos, the emanating power of God, in its dynamic aspect (as against the silent, inward aspect used in the Third Gate, where the Word just *is*, and no creature can alter or manipulate it).

In other words, there first exists the Creator Himself, the Logos, the great Creative Agent who utters the infinite pulsation of Sounding-Light Vibration, which, because of its infinite nature, does not actually create any *thing*. This is where the Creative Hierarchies come in. It is the Elohīm who modulated that *omnific Vibration* to make their own Mantra of Creation, which they used to create the Worlds. Unfortunately the Jewish Rabbis wrongly translated Elohīm as "God", but the Elohīm are not one God but a plurality of Creator Gods, extraordinarily advanced Creative Intelligences who uttered the Word (Mantra) of Creation whereby all things came into being.

This also happens when your Soul creates your personality. When your physical body dies your consciousness moves into your astral body; when the astral body dies your consciousness moves into your mental body; and when your mental body dies your consciousness moves into your Soul. But then nothing further can happen; you can't reincarnate. In order to reincarnate, you as a Living Soul have to utter your creative word, a melodic sound known to you as a Soul. There is no Guru who can teach you that sound; it is your life, and you are uttering your Life Mantra.

As soon as you as a Living Soul send out that Mantra, you begin to gather the fine substance of the mental dimensions, forming a new mind body around you. As you repeat the next phase of your Mantra you form an astral body within the mental body, and then you repeat another phase of the Mantra and form the etheric-physical body. As a Soul, however, you cannot create for yourself a physical body. It is the earth processes which give you your physical body. So even as a Living Soul you have to create your own manifestation—*the Creative Word uttered by intelligent beings to bring forth a manifestation.* In your case, that manifestation is your own personality; in the case of the Elohīm, it is a planet, a sun or a solar system, depending on the level of attainment of those Cosmic Beings.

The Power of Active Sound

The power of Active Sound is not only in Mantra but also in other forms of sound:

MANTRA-ŚAKTI IS THE POWER OF ACTIVE SOUND IN MANTRAS, SPEECH AND MUSIC.

We refer to music here as Active Sound that carries an energy and has a rhythm you can hear with your physical ears. Music sends a message to your inner being and influences your emotional nature, your mind and your vital (pranic) body. In other words, your astral body, mental body and etheric-physical body (your life-force) change according to the music you listen to. This is something society is immensely ignorant of. Over the last forty years or so the pop music scene has produced an incredible amount of destructive, aggressive music that is causing a real problem for Mother Earth. Her planetary energy-field is controlled by energy vibrations, so when musicians scream, yell and smash their guitars, they destroy that energy-field; of course, when millions of young people listen and sing along, thinking it's cool, they add to the destruction.

Many musicians do not know that they are creators—they belong to one of the Creative Hierarchies—and should only be creating the good, the beautiful and the true. They are responsible either for the transformation of the planetary energy-field (by producing harmony) or for its destruction (by producing disharmony). Furthermore, when musicians create destructive or disharmonious music, the resulting energy-field rebounds on them and they will have a lot of negative karma to work out. This often starts with the destruction of their personal lives through the abuse of alcohol and drugs and leads to the destruction of their inner harmony, so when they die they go to a very unpleasant region of the Astral World, a region of dissonance and disharmony that they have to suffer and endure.

Speech is also creative or destructive because it is also dependent on Vibration. When we speak, the vocal cords produce a vibration expressed as sound, and the pattern or frequency of that vibration determines whether that speech is creative or destructive. Obviously if you're screaming and yelling at people, the energy pattern from your vocal box is destructive and adds to the destructive energy hitting the planet. People use the Creative Force, the power of Active Sound, all the time when they speak, but they have never been taught that speech is actually a *divine gift*, a gift from the Creator to Mankind, so they use it wrongly.

Many people talk themselves to death, quite literally, by speaking negatively about themselves. In the beginning it is just talk, a vibration created in the throat, but when it is repeated continually, the vibration materializes and becomes the real thing. What is more, you can create negative conditions not only for yourself but also for your family and your environment because the power of Sound is limitless. On the other hand, if you talk positively all the time it changes the existing condition into a more positive condition—Nature will begin to help you, She will give you more power and energy to do things and you will be guided from the Inside.

This is something people should learn at school, instead of all the useless stuff they are taught, because it is part of what I call the essentials you must know as a human being on this planet, the kind of knowledge that shapes human life and destiny. We are creators and we create through music, through speech and through Mantra.

The reason behind the power of Mantra or the power of music or the power of speech—the power of Sound—is this:

Vibration is the basis of all Existence.

This is the Fundamental Law of the Cosmos: everything in Creation is continually in a state of Vibration. Even rocks, which are apparently solid, are actually moving. If you had transdimensional vision and could see the structure of matter, you would see an incredibly furious activity going on all the time. The only reason we don't see this movement is because of the cosmic force that makes every form stay in its particular shape, making things seem solid, stable and unmoving. We call it the *Archetypal Pattern Force* and it makes a human being look like a human being, an angel look like an angel, an animal look like an animal. It is a tremendous Power-field in the Divine Mind that maintains everything in the Cosmos according to a plan and pattern. Without it, there would be total chaos in the Cosmos; but within it, there is continuous movement.

Since Vibration is the basis of all existence, therefore, it follows that when we work with Mantra-Śakti we are working with Vibration. Why? Because Mantra is Vibration and the Power of Mantra is a science that allows us to *change* vibration. Remember, by Mantra-Śakti we can produce new manifestations or change the vibration of already existing things. This is where the science comes in, because as a human being you have a basic rate of vibration that will not lead you to the Path of Unfoldment, just as a tree has a certain basic rate of vibration that will never allow the tree to reach Buddhic Consciousness. Every rate of vibration has its own particular set of limitations.

Which brings us to the next layer of understanding of the Esoteric Science of Mantra:

THE MAGIC OF THE CURRENT OF CONSTANT ATTENTION ACTUALIZES THE REAL.

Your attention is like a current, like a moving reality, and when you are fixed on one particular mantric pattern or sequence, it actualizes the Real. Suppose your mantra is to Śiva or Buddha or Christ, or to the Universal Light Vibration. In the beginning you just know that Śiva, Rama, Christ, God or whatever aspect of the Cosmic Manifestation you want to reach is "out there". It's not real to you at that stage. But as you repeat the mantra or chant, focusing on it, a current of attention is set up on the inner dimensions between you and that reality. And as you keep repeating the mantra, that current increases until the Real *happens*, which means that you identify with that which you first thought was "out there"; you and It become one.

The longer you repeat the mantra or chant, the stronger will be your connection with that other reality—*which is always there*. The Buddha is always there, the Christ is always there, God is always there; but your attention is not directed to them and therefore you cannot experience them. So when you work with the Mantra-Śakti, the Way of Divine Sound, your attention is focused and your concentration builds up until it actually touches the Real. Then your attention switches from yourself to *That*, and you are in the state of Yoga, Union, Oneness or integration with the object of your worship. This is the ultimate understanding of this Science: the magic of the current of constant attention actualizes the Real.

Mantra Repetition in the Third-Eye Centre:

ŌṀ NAMŌ ŌṀ NAMAḤ

This is an active meditation whereby you *physically* intone the Sanskrit sound-structure ŌṀ NAMŌ ŌṀ NAMAḤ in a manner that focuses the Light-energy in your Third-Eye Cakra. You simply close your eyes, focus in the Third-Eye Cakra (not the physical brain but slightly in front of the area between the eyes) and intone aloud the sound-structure ŌṀ NAMŌ ŌṀ NAMAḤ. After intoning it aloud for a short while, continue intoning it silently in the Third Eye with the same purposeful, steady rhythm.

It is best to first intone the mantra physically, aloud, so that the brain picks up that vibration. Then, when you intone it silently the vibration goes from your brain to your mind, so the mind becomes harmonized and stabilized. When you listen to one pop song after another your attention is moving on all the time and there is no continuum of attention. With the Science of Mantra, however, you focus your energy on a mantric sequence and keep your energy and your attention on it. And that is what brings you to the amazing state of Unity, or integration with the Divine.[13]

---

[13] An audio file demonstrating the intonation of this mantra can be found at www.planetary-transformation.org/mantrarepetition

THE SIXTH GATE

THE WAY OF
COSMIC LOVE

The Cosmic Heart

The Way of Cosmic Love, also called *the Way of Devotion*, is a universal Way. Millions of people over the centuries followed this Path, because, whichever religion they belonged to, the basic principle of that religion was *devotion*. So the Devotional Path was the life of the planet for thousands of years, but people didn't understand it as a Way and they followed it without the scientific understanding of *what* they were doing and *why* they were doing it.

Since the time of Atlantis the Way of Cosmic Love has been *the* Way for Humanity because since then the emphasis has been on *human emotions*, developing the Solar Plexus Centre (the Feeling Centre) and the Heart Centre (the Spiritual Feeling Centre). But this is going to change now, because now the emphasis is on the *mind*, awakening the Third-Eye Centre and the Crown Centre. Development of the mind started around the time of the Buddha and has been steadily increasing since then. As you know, compulsory education nowadays revolves around the mind, so the human attention has moved from the Solar Plexus and Heart Centres to the Third-Eye and Crown Centres.

But it is impossible to understand the Way of Cosmic Love through the mind; no intellectual training can help you understand it because the Mind Principle is a different principle. That is why we have to give you the fundamentals of this Path, the Way of Cosmic Love—the most beautiful way of life for a human being on this planet. What is more, unless you can walk this Path of Devotion, you will never become a real human being. For what makes you a human being is the Heart.

We will first bring it down to a level where it can be easily understood, because saying *Cosmic Love* is fine but it's very far away. (It isn't really but it *seems* far away.) We will start with this one point, a fundamental clue for you to understand the Heart and its significance in your life:

THE HEART GENERATES AN INTELLIGENT FORCE THAT GIVES A POSITIVE QUALITY TO LIFE.

People who are totally intellectual and have no Heart activity are in a state of what we would call "perpetual mental depression", because the mental faculty does not give you a quality of life; it is simply a faculty, a faculty of the mind. This is why some scientists, brilliant though they may be, can still perform the most startling acts of cruelty, like experimenting on living animals. They work with the mind without any emotional feeling, and this sometimes can result in cruelty or a total disrespect for life, simply because they have no Heart—just like the existential philosophers who say that life is meaningless and when it's over, that's it! Kaput! They too are dead in the Heart.

That the Heart gives a positive quality to life can be applied to anybody, whether you are religious or not; you don't necessarily have to believe in God or be a good Roman Catholic, Jew, Muslim, Hindu or Buddhist. If you have an awakened Heart, you are a human being.

Here is an example of what I mean. When I was a child in Hungary during the communist days I sometimes visited my relatives in Slovakia. Although they lived in desperately poor conditions, they gave you the best they could, and you always felt a warmth emanating from them. That warmth is the Heart. It was not an intellectual quality, not an intellectual decision to treat their relatives well; it was a feeling of togetherness and oneness, a force that made you feel good.

When your Heart is open, the way you look at life is different and you can put things in a positive context even in the face of starvation, sickness or other negative circumstance. You can't do that when you are in your mind. Observe yourself and other people and you will discover the simple fact that anybody who has their Heart open has a positive radiation coming from them—a small radiation if the Heart is open a little bit and a much larger radiation if it is open more. Now, imagine if you open your Heart completely and link it to the Cosmic Heart, the Heart of the Christ. Then what? How powerful will that Heart be for the *good*, for creating a positive quality to all life!

The next layer of understanding, the next principle in the Way of Cosmic Love is:

DEVOTION ATTRACTS THE BELOVED.

Have you ever had a girlfriend or a boyfriend? Did you notice that if you didn't have devotion to him or her, they wouldn't notice that you exist? If you don't have devotion to the other, the other will have nothing to do with you. Devotion attracts the beloved, whoever the beloved is. If your beloved is a cat or a dog or a horse, the animal will come to you because you are devoted to it and the animal feels that and responds. Devotion connects you to the object of your devotion, like sending a text message connects you to the other person. I'm using examples on the human level that you can understand, because on the cosmic level it is exactly the same: *Devotion to God attracts God to you.* If you don't have devotion to God, therefore, you don't attract God; God leaves you alone. That might explain why God is not coming to you.

Now we will go a bit deeper into the understanding of the Heart, that it is not only part of our humanness but is also more profound than that:

THE HEART IS THE SEAT OF THE LOVE-WISDOM ENERGY.

When the Heart is awakened to the Inner Worlds, to higher levels of consciousness, it becomes a field of energy that emanates the Principle of Love and Wisdom. To give an example, in Chinese Taoism many of the Sages did not teach in a school setting but in a temple setting. (The School, or Ashram, and the Temple are different ways of giving out knowledge.) In Taoist temples, the emphasis was not on revealing knowledge, not on teaching principles and ideas, but on simply being there. The disciples lived in the temple with the Sage, sitting in meditation every day, chopping wood, fetching water, and over the years they developed the faculty of awakening the Heart and going into the state of Enlightenment. In other words, in that process of living with the Sage, the radiation of Enlightenment was slowly communicated to them.

This means that the Heart of those Sages emanated the Love-Wisdom energy because the Heart is the storehouse of Love and Wisdom, the two aspects of Buddhic Consciousness. Such Sages radiate an innate Love and an innate Wisdom, so whether they say anything or not you still get that energy from them, and that energy harmonizes you. It works on its own even if you don't understand what it is doing.

Now we are getting to a more cosmic level, a Sanskrit word you may have heard of—BHAKTI.

BHAKTI IS DEVOTION, FAITH, LOVE AND SURRENDERING YOUR EGO TO GOD.

Bhakti is usually defined as "devotion to God", but it is actually a multidimensional experience of Devotion, Faith, Love and Surrendering your ego to God. When you are devoted to the Deity, you have all of these qualities.

Devotion is actually born inside us. When we are children we are devotional, we have faith and we believe in miracles, in Jesus Christ, in Santa Claus. We believe that there *is* a Deity, that there *are* wonderful things in the Cosmos, that the angels *can* come and talk to us and life *can* be beautiful. That innocent belief is actually an aspect of Devotion and comes from an inner recognition of the Truth, that there is something outside of ourselves that is beautiful, wonderful, true, divine. But as we become educated and learn how things work, that simple faith disappears from our consciousness. Yet maintaining that simple faith will actually open the Gate to Cosmic Love.

In the Way of Cosmic Love we re-establish ourselves in that state of wonder which we call *Faith*. It may be faith in the Christ, the Buddha, Kṛṣṇa, Rāma, the Deity or in the Father, Son and Holy Ghost; faith in a Divine Intelligence, in the Solar Logos; faith in something beyond us, something larger, something infinite, something more wonderful. Such faith will begin to awaken a tremendous dynamic energy inside you because Faith is an actual *energy*, not just an idea.

Intellectuals like to debate about whether or not God exists, and they give all kinds of reasons why or why not, but it is all just fluff of the mind. But with Faith, you *know* that there is a God; you *know* that the Christ exists, that Buddha exists, that Kṛṣṇa, Rāma, Lao-Tzu, Moses and Mohammed were real. How people portray these beings, how they philosophize about them doesn't matter. The mind tries to explain things but you know that with or without the mind these things are *real*. Faith tells you that, and it produces an energy current inside you that lifts your life-wave to a higher level. And because that energy comes from the Heart, you can't necessarily explain what you are feeling or why. You just look at a sunset and are struck by its beauty.

I was born with Devotion, Faith and Love and I still can't understand a person who doesn't feel that there is another wonderful reality beyond this physical world. I can't comprehend what that consciousness could be like because to me it is like being annihilated or living in total restriction. People who are a hundred percent materialistic live in that consciousness, without Devotion, Faith or Love. Chairman Mao said, "Religion is the poison of the people!" So every religious sentiment had to be destroyed, which means that Devotion, Faith and Love had to be destroyed. That is typical communism, typical materialism—destroying the wonder of life.

A scientist looks at a flower and identifies its chemical compounds and explains how they work, but that does not explain why the flower looks so beautiful or how it arranged its various atoms to form a perfect six-pointed star. It is the same with the Cosmos: the scientific idea is that all the substance in the Cosmos was put together (nobody knows how) and then exploded to give us this wonderful universe. So the substance exploded, but why did it form itself into galaxies? Why did the galaxies form stars and the stars form planets, and why are there beings on this planet? Of course, you can give a scientific explanation but that is a non-explanation, because the reason the flower can form itself into a perfect geometric design is because there is a

Divine Intelligence that works through geometry. And the reason the Cosmos is organized is because it is the work of an organized Mind in Creation that ensures there is Intelligence behind everything from the largest scale right down to the structure of the atom. Every form in Nature is simply the Divine Mind in action, and the Mind of God always produces beauty; and therefore the flowers are beautiful, the animals are beautiful, the stars are beautiful.

Now, you may have been born with faith, love and devotion toward the Deity as an innate tendency, but when you begin to consciously follow the Path, then you have to *surrender your ego to God*. And that is when it *really* becomes the Way of Cosmic Love.

Surrendering your ego is what makes you a Saint in the true sense of the word, as against a Sage. A Sage is a Knower, a Jñāni, one who *knows* through the Wisdom of the Heart, whereas a Saint is one who has the Love of the Heart. They are very different. Within your Heart is the ego, that structure inside you that says, I want this; I want that; I am this; I am that. Your ego is your personal self which communicates with your environment and the world, whereby you are able to live in the world and do things. Before you can carry out the Way of Cosmic Love, a major change has to take place in that ego structure.

The beginning stage of this change is difficult. There can be huge conflicts because your human ego wants to carry on its activity as normal while at the same time you are experiencing impulses coming from deeper in the Heart. The first impulses are what we call *conscience*—you realize that you did something wrong and feel unhappy about it, not because the government or the laws of the country say so but because inside your Heart you feel that it is wrong. This is simply a manifestation of the Divine Presence inside you trying to teach you something, and it means that your personal ego is beginning to break up, that it no longer has that strong iron determination for everything to be done according to how you want it done.

As your Cosmic Love increases, the ego breaks up more and more and you become more aware of your actions and reactions, and this is where guilt comes in. You realize that you shouldn't have done something and feel sorry for yourself. But this is only a transitory stage because when the Heart fully opens you will know three things: one, that you function in this world; two, that you are not perfect; and three, that the Path is an ever-continuous readjustment, that is, your Heart is continuously readjusting to this world and the next world. In fact, at the level of Cosmic Love the Heart functions simultaneously in the two directions of the Cross: upwardly toward the Divine and horizontally toward the world. And you are literally crucified on the Cross.

In the Bible, the crucifixion of Christ is a symbol of someone whose Heart is embracing the Divine, the Cosmic Love aspect, and at the same time is enmeshed in the actual living processes of Creation; someone, therefore, who is crucified continually between what should be done outwardly and what should be done inwardly, alternating between the inner and outer dimensional realities. And this involves pain. A good example that illustrates this is the story of Jesus in the Garden of Gethsemane. He knew that He was going to be seized by the authorities, and He didn't want that—His *ego* didn't want that. He saw no point in it: why be destroyed by those stupid religious and worldly materialists? He went through this process in his human heart, the heart that functions on the horizontal arm of the Cross, but then His Heart functioned on the other arm of the Cross, the vertical arm, and He said, "Let Your Will be done, not mine" (MATTHEW 26: 42). This is a momentous occasion that shows that even the Christ struggled with His human nature and His divine nature.

The Way of the Mystic, which is part of the Way of Cosmic Love, involves a similar struggle. If you read about Saints such as St Teresa, St John of the Cross, Meister Eckhart or St Suso, you will find that their lives were a battle between their relationship to the human condition and their relationship to the Divine Condition within. And that battle raged on until they finally gave up their ego completely and were in the condition of "Let Your Will be done, not mine"; until the human will no longer had significance for them and they would do exactly what the Divine Impulse coming through them wanted them to do. If it meant hard work, they would do it; if it meant travelling somewhere, they would do it. They followed the Divine Impulse at terrific personal cost, totally sacrificing themselves.

As mentioned previously, the Way of Cosmic Love is one of the most beautiful and exalted Paths on the planet. As you go deeper into this Path, in spite of all the suffering and problems you may encounter, you will realize that there is a sea of Infinite Bliss inside you and that you live in that Ecstasy all the time.

DEVOTION IS THE CAUSE OF BLISS CONSCIOUSNESS.

Some Muslim Saints were beaten and tortured, persecuted in horribly cruel ways, as were some of the ancient Jewish Prophets and Christian Saints. (For some reason these three religions, the Christian, Muslim and Jewish religions, were very cruel in their dealings with Saints. The Buddhist and Hindu Saints were much better off.) These Saints had to go through the outer suffering because the religious and worldly authorities were against them. Remember, the more Light you give out, the more you attract the Opposition; that is the Law. The *religious* authorities were particularly bad; they went to church every day, worshipped God every day and yet they were immensely cruel to the Saints. I do not understand how those two things can exist together, being so cruel when you are supposed to be a religious person.

But regardless of the outer circumstances the Saints found themselves in, they lived in a state of absolute Bliss Consciousness. They would still register the pain of the cruelty, of course, but they would immerse themselves in that overwhelming Bliss, which is an indescribable condition far beyond joy or happiness. It was their reward on the Way of Cosmic Love and they live in that condition as a permanent state of being. So in spite of the difficulties of the Path—the struggle between the human self and the Divine Self and the persecution by the authorities—there is nevertheless an unending ocean of Bliss as the reward of the Way of Cosmic Love, and that reward is forever.

The Heart Mantra

KLĪṀ KṚṢṆĀYA

GOVINDĀYA

GOPĪJANA

VALLABHĀYA

SVĀHĀ

This is a Heart Initiation that awakens the flame of Divine Love in your heart. It is really the Mantra of the Christ in Sanskrit, except that it predates the Christ by 2,500 years.

I will first explain why it is important to use Sanskrit, rather than, say, an English translation. When you work in Sanskrit you are using the energy of the Sanskrit language, which has the power of Light. If you say the Mantra in English, you have the thought of what it means but there is no Mantric Energy, no Mantra-Śakti involved. In Sanskrit you have the thought as well as the *power* of the sound, the power of the Sanskrit language to bring Light.

Another reason we use Sanskrit is because it has a direct connection to the energy of Love. This Mantra is from the time when Kṛṣṇa, the previous incarnation of the Christ, was in incarnation. The Divine Being who embodies the Love aspect of the Deity comes into incarnation at certain times to bring that Love-energy into human consciousness on a planetary scale. Kṛṣṇa did that, the Christ did that, and the next incarnation will be an Avatāra called Maitreya, who will do the same thing.

Now I'll explain the meaning of each word of the Heart Mantra.[14]

---

[14] An audio file demonstrating the intonation of this mantra can be found at www.planetary-transformation.org/mantrarepetition

KLĪṀ is the power of Attraction. We mentioned previously that unless you have that energy of devotion, you cannot connect your consciousness to the Deity and therefore there is no contact established. Klīṁ, in the Sanskrit sound structure, is that connecting link. When you say "Klīṁ", it is like calling or texting a friend, except that it is more direct and the 'friend' is Kṛṣṇa.

KṚṢṆA is the Sanskrit word for the "Christ". When the Greek Sages went to India they called Kṛṣṇa *Christos*, which later became *Christ*. The ending *āya* is the dative form of the noun, meaning "*to Kṛṣṇa*". So with the first two words of the Mantra we are making a connection to the Principle of Love, which is Kṛṣṇa (Christ), the embodiment of the Heart of God.

GOVINDA means "one who guides the Souls" and Govindāya means "to Govinda, the guider of Souls". We are referring here to the Way of the Mystic (which belongs to the Way of Cosmic Love), and for the Mystic, the Love-energy of the Deity is the guiding force.

GOPĪJANA are the people of the Way of Devotion, the Saints and devotees who devote their life to God. Notice there is no specification of country or religion to which these people belong. In Old Testament times they were called the "People of the Way", which referred to any person from any race who followed the Way of Bhakti (Devotion to God).

VALLABHĀYA means "to the Beloved". The term *the Beloved* has been used by the Jewish, Christian, Muslim and Hindu Mystics to refer to the Deity, mainly the loving aspect of the Divine Presence.

SVĀHĀ is equivalent to 'hanging up the phone'. So with Klīṁ you 'dial up' the loving Heart of the Deity, the Beloved, who is the guiding force for all the people engaged in the Way of Devotion, the Way of Cosmic Love, from every race in every country and every time, and then with Svāhā you 'hang up'.

About This Technique

When the Guru initiates you into this Mantra (because this is an Initiatory Mantra, you have to be properly initiated[15]) then several things happen. As the Guru chants the Mantra, a star gate in the form of a five-pointed star forms in the Heart Centre of the Guru, and then as the Mantra is repeated that five-pointed star begins to glow and expand in Inner Space, becoming like a funnel. At a certain point there comes a response through that funnel—a shaft of Divine Love-energy from the Christ (Kṛṣṇa) or from the Heart of the Deity, the Heart of the Solar Logos. Having different qualities from the Light-energy of the GĀYATRĪ MANTRA, which comes from another part of the Deity, the energy of Divine Love then spreads outwards to the people being initiated, and as they recite the Mantra, the same five-pointed star forms inside each person and then above the group, and that energy floods the group and works in the Heart of each person.

If this Mantra is practised at home, it will keep opening the Heart Cakra, creating that funnel effect through which the downpour of Divine Grace will come. Whether the Christ (Kṛṣṇa) actually enters your Heart depends on how far you go in the process. When it happens, you will realize that the Christ figure (or the Kṛṣṇa figure) is only an object of worship to focus your attention on, and beyond it you will feel the real Divine Love like a dynamic torrent of energy.

Don't worry if you cannot remember the meaning of the words. Just think of the Christ or Kṛṣṇa, or have in your mind the thought of the loving energy that emanates from the Heart of God. If you remember the meaning of the words, then have that in your mind, but the important thing is that you *feel* the energy of the Mantra pulsating in your Heart.

---

[15] See "Note on Initiation" on page 173.

*****

The Heart Mantra is actually a Holy Communion device. In the Christian church, the Holy Communion is the part of the Mass where the priest says the magic words and the wine and host are consecrated and then given to the people to drink and eat. The original idea behind this, however, was that when the priest said the magic words, the Love-energy of the Christ would descend into those substances through the priest, who would then give that Love-energy to the people. That was in the days when the priests understood what they were doing. But nowadays what do they do? They say the prayers and get the wafers and wine from a cupboard and give them to the people—totally unconsecrated. This is because the church and the priests think the ritual is just in memory of the Last Supper of Christ, without understanding that it is in fact a divine magic, that the Eucharist was originally intended to be a *holy communion with the Divine Presence*.

The Heart Mantra is the essence of the 'magic words' (mantric sequence) that bring down the Love-energy of the Christ for the Holy Communion, but the only difference is that you don't have to consume any outer substance because you are invoking the Divine Presence directly into yourself; therefore, you don't need the external ritual of the Mass invented by the priests. This Mantra is the communion part of that ritual, a *true* Holy Communion, exactly how it was in the early days of Christianity when the disciples said the magic words and received the Christ-force, the presence of the Christ.

*****

If you feel a pain in your heart while practising this meditation, don't worry about it; it's quite normal. Have you ever seen a picture of the Christ with His heart burning? Well that represents the suffering of the Christ, but on a cosmic level. His Heart is burning for the whole planet, not just for you. We call it the *Cosmic Heart* because He follows the Way of Cosmic Love, so whatever He experiences is cosmic and vast in dimension.

Note on Initiation

Within our Spiritual Hierarchy there are Adepts and Masters who have the Mantra-Śakti, that is to say, who have the inborn ability to use mantras to bring about transformation in human consciousness and in the planetary consciousness. These cosmic-intelligent beings follow a particular line of evolution, whether it is the human evolutionary line, angelic evolutionary line or the evolutionary line of the gods, and the very essence of their life-force, meaning and destiny is to use the Creative Word in the form of powerful mantric sounds to bring about manifestations or transform existing conditions. With regard to the human evolutionary line, some Masters or Adepts may use Knowledge, Wisdom or Devotion, but the Masters of Mantra belong to a particular hierarchy that specifically works with the Creative Word, and they are constituted accordingly.

It is for this reason that only a Guru who has the Mantra-Śakti can initiate people into a mantra, because only he or she has the energy or power of that mantra and can transfer that energy to a person through the process of *Initiation*. The Creative Word is omnific, consisting of many vibrations, and Initiation is the transference of a certain vibration of the Creative Word that human beings can work with on this physical level. (The angels and the other hierarchies use other vibrations that are suitable for them.) You cannot get that same energy from a mantra in a book; you have to have a living Guru, a living Teacher, otherwise it doesn't work.

So at the time of Initiation, you receive an energy and that force is communicated to you in what we call the form or the frame of the mantric sequence. The energy is transferred into your causal body and it is kept alive as you practise the mantra. (The more you practise it, the more it is kept alive.) And then what happens is that, as already mentioned in the previous chapter, a continuum of attention is established that connects you to where that mantra is directed, because every mantra is directed to a specific part of Reality. As you keep practising it, you get closer and closer until you finally—boom!—connect to that particular reality.

The Guru, or the person who has the Mantra-Śakti, can also nominate Initiators. An Initiator is one who has already received the Initiation from the Guru beforehand and he or she has been practising along that Mantric Energy line and has attained a certain experience of it. It's not necessary that they have had the complete experience, because while they practise they are connected to the Teacher's energy-field and through that they can initiate. The Mantric Energy is conveyed from the Guru's energy-field through the Initiator's auric field to the new person being initiated.

But then there arises the question of what happens when the Guru leaves this world, for then we are left with only the Initiators. When the Guru dies, the first layer of Initiators, whom we could call apostles or disciples, can hand down the energy to the next lot of people and, if they are still in tune with the Teacher internally, can empower the second generation of Initiators. By this time, however, the energy-field of the Guru has started to fizzle out because the Guru is moving up the planes, so by the time the energy transference gets to the second generation, it is very weak and by the end of the second generation the energy-field is practically negligible.

If the Teacher died centuries ago, there are no actual Initiators, no real energy transmission in the group, so it is what I would call a philosophical group or a religious group. For instance, in the Christian religion, the twelve disciples were the first generation and conveyed the energy to the next group of people; after that, however, it fizzled out and the highly esoteric knowledge-field of the Christ was lost by the time the church was established. It was the same with the Buddha. He originally had four hundred pupils and they initiated several hundreds more, but by the third generation the essence of the Buddha's teaching had been lost. If you want to become a follower of the Buddha or the Christ, you can do that, but it is not an *energy-reality*; it is a philosophical, religious or theological reality. To get an energy-reality, the reality of Mantra, you have to go to a living Teacher.

THE WAY OF TRANSMISSION
OF DIVINE POWER

The Seventh Gate is *The Way of the Transmission of Divine Power*. Another word for it in Sanskrit is GURUKULA, which means the "family of the Guru". This is a Gate that you cannot follow because the necessary circumstances are not available to you. It is an ancient way, much practised in India for thousands of years, as well as in China (where the word *Sage, Teacher* or *Adept* is used) and in some of the Jewish mystical circles. Basically, it means that if you wanted to become spiritually enlightened, you went to live in the household of a Guru and became a member of his family, which may have consisted of the Guru's wife, children and other relatives, as well as other disciples who wanted to become enlightened.

Some Gurus were married, because in those days a Guru didn't have to be celibate or shun interaction with the world. That idea came later, but that is not the True Way and never has been; the idea that you have to be a monk to follow the Spiritual Path is unnatural. Many Gurus had children and the disciples would help with the children as they were growing up, as in normal family life. The age of the disciple didn't matter, although it was usually young students who wanted to become enlightened who would ask if they could live with the Guru.

They started their spiritual journey in this way, spending ten, fifteen or twenty years in the household of the Guru.

This system is not structured like a school that has regular lessons or like an ashram where you live with a large number of people, each having a particular job to do. One drawback of this system was (and still is) that Gurus usually had very few disciples because only a few people could live in their household, so they didn't really help many people. It is quite different in the Ashram system, where there is a possibility for hundreds of people to become enlightened, or in the School system, which offers that possibility to even more people.

The School system originally came from the idea of living with a Teacher until you became perfected. Many Chinese Taoist and Japanese Zen Schools were founded by disciples who had lived in the aura of the Master and then established their school after they became enlightened. In the Ashram system, a modern example of this is Ramana Mahārṣi, who originally lived in a cave at Mount Arunachala in Tiruvannamalai, following the old Gurukula system. People who wanted to follow him started living with him and, lo and behold, forty years later he had a huge ashram.

The Guru (Adept, Sage or Teacher) has a subtle, expansive energy-field that radiates energy, or Divine Power. The Guru emanates Divine Power all the time, whether sleeping or awake, because it is the Soul of the Guru, not the Guru's personality, that transmits the Divine Power. The Guru's energy-field is multidimensional, penetrating the Physical, Astral, Mental and Causal Worlds, so if you live in the household of the Guru you are naturally immersed in that energy-field and the radiation of the Divine Power impacts on your own auric field. Your outer and inner mechanisms—your body, emotions, mind and your Soul—are transformed by a natural process of radiation of Divine

Power. The transformation is not drastic, not like being suddenly hit by lightning, but gradual and natural, without any stress or effort on the part of the student.

In this type of system the Guru did not normally give the students any spiritual instruction. There are many stories of students who grew tired of chopping wood and doing all the hard work year in and year out, complaining that they weren't even given a mantra. The students didn't realize that being in the presence of the Guru was *the* thing—not all the other stuff—that they were already in the process of Enlightenment.

In the Way of Transmission of Power, therefore, the Guru transmits the Power in a natural way and the disciple receives the radiation or emanation coming from the Guru. Of course, in the modern world we can't follow this Way because the whole structure of society has changed. The system is no longer operational but I mention it because it exists and is still possible, if you can find an Enlightened Master who will allow you to live with him or her.

THE WAY OF SUDDEN GRACE/ BY THE UNIVERSAL OUTPOURING OF THE SPIRIT

The Eighth Gate to Enlightenment is another Path that you cannot follow. There are two ways it can open for you: through the Way of Sudden Grace or by the Universal Outpouring of the Spirit.

The first part is the *Way of Sudden Grace*. You may have read the story of Saul who became St Paul. He was a bad person who used to round up Christians to be killed. He was on the way to Damascus one day when suddenly the Light hit him and physically blinded him. He had a rebirth and became *the* champion of Christianity for all time. It was Paul who organized the church and became the teacher of teachers of Christianity.

There are many examples of this among the Christian Saints. In the early days of Christianity, for instance, there were violent robbers who used to rob people throughout the countryside, even the monks who were meditating in the desert. There was one robber who robbed an old monk who had very few possessions to begin with, taking everything the monk owned except his food bowl. When he left, the old monk ran after him, calling out, "Here, take my food bowl as well. Take everything!" What happened then was—Sudden Grace. The old monk was a highly spiritual person and when he gave up the last thing he owned on earth, something hit the robber and converted him into a Christian who not only gave up his lifestyle of robbing but also went into the desert, started meditating and attained sainthood.

In the East, too, there are many stories of gangs of robbers (called "dacoits") who robbed the rich, and some of the greatest dacoits became well-known Gurus whom people worshipped as great holy men and who founded religions in India.

These are examples of the Way of Sudden Grace and they show this Way is not something that a person deserves or is wanting or looking for. Often the recipients can be the biggest sinners, violent people who have committed many crimes, but in their good fortune they come across a real Saint, somebody who has the magic power inside them, and they become converted, just like that. In other words, the Divine Consciousness itself intervenes and, through that holy person, gives the sinner an opportunity to equalize their negative karmas and be liberated in that lifetime—not for the sake of that one person but *for what that one person can do for Mankind.*

So the Way of Sudden Grace is one part of the Eighth Gate and it works by Divine Mercy, the compassionate aspect of the Heart of the Deity. The other part of the Eighth Gate, the other way it opens, is: *by the Universal Outpouring of the Spirit.* Here the Divine Grace is not poured out onto one person but all of Mankind, that is, the whole energy-field of the planet is used as an inlet for the Divine Grace. This was the case at the time of the Buddha and at the time of the Christ, and the same thing is happening now, with the coming of the Planetary Avatāra.

The Universal Outpouring is an extra-Solar Systemic energy from the very Heart of the Deity, what we call the Heart-Power of the Deity, a massive, radiating energy-field bombarding and embracing the whole planet with the power of Love and Wisdom. This tremendous power is already here, the energy of Love and Wisdom is already penetrating the normal planetary structure, but very few people can sense it. Over the next thirty to fifty years, however, it will increase because of the New Avatāra. Anyone who has an inner sensitivity and can sense this extra-phenomenal, extra-material energy—and can embrace it—will be liberated and enter the Eighth Gate to Eternal Life. It doesn't matter whether they are Christian, Buddhist, Muslim, Communist or Capitalist. Their worldly situation or religious background has nothing to do with it; it has to do with the ability to receive finer vibrations, like the new spiritual impulse of the Coming Avatāra.

The Christ explained this in an interesting way. He said that if a family is working in the field when the Outpouring comes, "one will be taken and three will be left" (LUKE 17: 36). He was saying that whoever can receive the Outpouring of the Spirit will be "taken", that is, transformed and liberated in that moment. The energy-field of the Universal Outpouring will go right through the whole planet and thousands, maybe even millions, of people will be able to ab-sorb it, depending on their *preparation*. At the time of the Christ, St John said, "Prepare and make way for the coming of the Lord!" (MATTHEW 3: 3). Notice he said *prepare*. He knew about the coming Universal Outpouring of the Spirit and was trying to warn people to prepare themselves for that momentous event, because if they were sufficiently prepared they would receive that energy, be swamped by the Love of God and be liberated.

The more prepared people there are, the greater will be the pos-sibility for the Avatāra to transform the planet. But herein lies the problem with materialism: materialistic people do not prepare them-selves because they do not even believe in spiritual things. So they do not regenerate their vibration and will not be able to receive the Universal Outpouring.

You cannot do much about the Way of Sudden Grace because it is beyond you; it is a gift of God. But you *can* do something about the Universal Outpouring, by preparing yourself. Simply work and follow any one of the Ways we have described and that will purify you, by which we mean it will lift your vibration beyond its present range within your normal life. So when the Universal Outpouring increases, your whole internal mechanism will swing into the rhythm of the energy of the Coming Avatāra, and you will feel the transformation inside because that energy works by restructuring your cakras. Then you will feel yourself literally reborn, made into a new creation, and you will attain Liberation, Immortality.

I hope this will inspire you to do something in the here and now, because much depends on you. Due to the economy of Nature, the Avatāric Energy will not bombard the planet forever. There is a certain cycle: it increases until it reaches its maximum and then it becomes weaker and weaker until it disappears, just like at the time of the Christ, when the inner energies were strong for three years and then slowly withdrew. People still don't understand what planetary transformation is about. It is not a transformation of the outer physical conditions of the planet; that is only one result of it. The planet has to be transformed on the inside first—and similarly, the human being has to be transformed on the inside first—before any outer physical transformation can take place.

THE NINTH GATE

THE WAY OF
VISUALIZING THE REAL

Strangely enough, the Way of Visualizing the Real is the most widely used Gate, employed daily by millions of people, and the least known and understood—which is why people do not achieve Enlightenment in large numbers. So we will explain why this is a Cosmic Gate and how you can use it to attain Eternal Life.

Each of these Nine Paths is based on Cosmic Law (how the Cosmos works) and how human beings are related to the workings of the Cosmos, and for each of these Paths there are principles that give you an overall understanding of what the Law is about. Fundamental to understanding this beautiful path, the Way of Visualizing the Real, is this first principle:

THE MIND IS THE IMAGE-MAKING FACULTY. THEREFORE, THE MIND CAN BE CONTROLLED BY IMAGES, PICTURES AND SYMBOLS.

Let us start with the level of ordinary understanding. Firstly, you have a mind—*which is not the brain*. If you think that your mind is your brain, then you will not understand this Path. The mind *uses* the brain, which is just a physical instrument, a contact point to enable you to function in the physical body in the physical world. The mind itself is something else. The mind is the mental body, which is made of subtle matter much finer than physical matter and finer still than emotional (astral) matter. Now, your mind, your mental body, has an image-making faculty. In fact, to make images is *the* faculty of the mind, and because we all have it, every human being on this planet can be liberated through the Ninth Gate, if they can understand the science behind it.

So the first part of this principle is to acknowledge that the mind has an image-making faculty; the second part, however, is the real secret: *the mind can therefore be controlled by images, pictures and symbols.* This is the key understanding that most people miss. Because your mind has that faculty, you can use that faculty to control your mind.

The whole idea of this part of the Esoteric Science is based on putting pictures, symbols and images in your mind. (The *science* is that you have to know what picture or symbol to use for what effect.) This is why esoteric groups have the Tarot Keys, Kabbalistic diagrams, Maṇḍalas, alchemical diagrams, and why people have holy pictures of Our Lady, Quan Yin, the Christ, the Buddha, Goddesses or Saints. The mind can be *controlled* by such images, symbols and pictures, and it is a most perfect and natural way of control because it does not involve taking drugs like LSD or prescribed medicines. You use the very faculty of the mind that everyone has and you don't have to introduce some external factor.

The minds of millions of people are out of control because they have not been taught that the mind can be controlled by putting the right picture into it. In fact, you can control your mind to absolute perfection and you can achieve anything, depending on the picture that you put into it. You can be a creative artist; you can be a great scientist; you can be an excellent politician; you can become a great Sage, Adept or Master; you can be anything—whatever you put into your mind, you become. This image-making faculty is the most beautiful and amazing faculty we have; it is a gift from God to Mankind.

So the first principle is that of control, you can control the mind by the very images and symbols the mind generates. The next principle says there is something you can do to *transform* your mind.

DESIRE-FUELLED MIND-IMAGES HAVE THE POWER TO TRANS-FORM YOUR LIFE AND MAKE IT GOD-LIKE OR HELLISH.

Again, this is something we all experience but we have not been told the truth behind it. The key here is *desire-fuelled mind-images*. An image in your mind that you continually desire has the power to transform your life for better or worse, depending on what the image is. In other words, you will either move up or down the scale of evolution depending on what kind of image you have in your mind and what degree of desire you project towards that image.

Have you ever met a husband and wife who look like each other? This happens when they each have a desire-fuelled image of the other in their minds. After a while those images blend together and the couple look the same and have the same way of talking and doing things. Some people have desire-fuelled mind-images to be like the Jedi Knights in the Star Wars movies, and they dress up and act like them. This also works in a negative way. For example, an innocent youth joins a street gang and becomes corrupted because he wants to be like the other gang members. He uses desire-fuelled mind-images to transform his life into a hellish life. Society is filled with desire-fuelled images and people gravitate towards them, either elevating or degrading themselves, depending on the image they desire.

The human mind has the image-making faculty *because* the Divine Mind functions in the same way:

GOD ALSO CREATES BY IMAGES (ARCHETYPES) IN THE COSMIC MIND. CREATIVE ART IS BASED ON IMAGINATION.

Once the Divine Mind starts creating images (which we technically call *archetypes*), those images become galaxies, solar systems, stars, planets, angelic beings, human beings—in a word, Reality. And as the Creative Mind of God keeps thinking, Evolution proceeds according to the perfect archetypes in the Divine Mind.

What God is can be scaled down to what a human being is, so all human faculties are the faculties of the Deity, except on a miniscule scale. On the human level, therefore, creative art is based on imagination. For instance, a potter who wants to create a beautiful vase has to first create it in his or her mind before materializing it physically. Similarly, before each great cycle of Universal Manifestation, the Mind of God forms an image of the next Universe and materializes that image into physical shape and form over billions of years of involution and devolution. It takes a long time to create Physical Manifestation, in the same way that it takes time for a potter who imagines a vase to create the physical vase.

The process is always the same: from a formless condition, an *intelligence* (whether human, angelic, planetary or Solar Logoic) begins to think and formulates from that nothingness an image of what is to be. From that image, a great Cosmic Creator (the Solar Logos) or a human being (an artist) begins to work to materialize that image in physical form.

So the creative arts—carving, sculpting, painting or any form of art that materializes something in the physical world—are based on the natural faculty of imagination. We all have this creative faculty, but not all we create leads to the Divine; some leads to hell. Some artists can be emotionally disturbed but still use the creative ability of the mind to create. There was an exhibition of a modern artist in a major American city a few years ago, and the gallery staff who were hanging the pictures felt the energy from those paintings to be so negative that they didn't want to be responsible for hanging them. Creative art is based on imagination, but we need to be aware of whether it produces a positive, inspiring energy or not.

This is the next law, the Law of Becoming:

WHAT YOU SEE, YOU BECOME.

Countries under the rule of a dictatorship often have pictures of the dictator everywhere—in school textbooks, in the news media, in public squares. That's because dictatorships are based on worship of the "glorious leader", who knows that people are influenced by seeing his picture everywhere and will then do exactly what he wants them to do. This principle is based on the fact that the Feminine Mind, which is generally called the subconscious mind, radiates outwardly and picks up whatever is in its surroundings. Your subconscious mind therefore picks up the energy of a picture in your house, and that energy influences you all of the time, even when you are in a different room. So if it's an unpleasant picture it influences you in an unpleasant way.

Here is an example. A South African family who had immigrated to New Zealand came to see me and told me that their new house had a terrible energy and asked me if I could do something about it. I told them I would first have to look at the place, because terrible energies can be generated by all kinds of negative forces. So I went to the house, which had a long hallway leading from the front door, and the first thing I noticed was that at the end of the hallway there was a carving of an African mask and a shield with two crossed spears on it. It was a souvenir they had brought back from Africa. What immediately hit me was that the mask and shield were full of an intensely negative, violent energy, because they probably had been used for rituals by a witch doctor or magician. I said, "I don't have to go any further, I know the solution to your problem." I advised them to take the carving off the wall and burn it. Although they were beautifully carved, the mask and shield had been used for wrong, evil purposes and were saturated with negative energy. The people burned them and their problems disappeared.

What is in your immediate environment is important because it has an influence upon you. In the material dimension, what you see, you become; but let us now take this principle further and apply it to the spiritual dimension.

SEEING THE IMAGE OF A DEITY, YOU BECOME THAT DEITY.

Practically all religions have holy pictures, sacred statues and images. Christianity has pictures of Saints, Our Lady and the Holy Trinity. Buddhism has pictures of Buddha. Hinduism has many images of Gods and Goddesses, such as Rama, Vishnu, Śivā and Kṛṣṇa. The idea behind having these sacred pictures or images is that by looking at them and meditating upon them, you become them.

This is the spiritualizing process of the Ninth Gate, the Way of Visualizing the Real, because when you see the image of a deity, you are seeing the Real. So how does the process work? If you have a particular image of a deity—whether it's the Christ, the Buddha, Kṛṣṇa, Rama, a saint or any Divine Incarnation—that picture radiates a certain quality, a certain transcendental energy, and even if you just have it in your environment you are bombarded with that energy. If you use the image as the object of a formal meditation, however, then naturally you link up to the energy-field of the image much faster.

We'll explain this meditation process in more detail because it is the spiritual science behind how to attain Liberation through the Ninth Gate. When you first meditate on the image of your chosen deity, which could also be a picture of your Guru, it transforms your mind and starts working to recreate you internally according to that image. Later there comes a higher stage where you actually become one with that image and come to act like that image. In other words, the imagination of a deity is a two-stage process:

STAGE 1 *Identification with an Image of the Deity*

STAGE 2 *Experience of the Transcendental, Formless Absolute*

There have been many arguments for thousands of years between those who believe that God has a form, that is, a personal God, and those who believe that God is formless, that is, impersonal or transcendental. Actually both arguments are correct.

When you identify yourself with an image of the Deity, you become that particular form, not another form. For example, if you visualize and meditate on the Christ, then you become like the Christ; if you visualize the Buddha, you become like the Buddha; and if you visualize Kṛṣṇa, you become identified with Kṛṣṇa. When the Mystics (of any religion) absorbed themselves into the image of their chosen Deity, identifying with the life, energy and reality of that image, they believed that they had reached their final goal—but they had only half-completed the Path. That's because God is boundless and absolute, not constricted to any form.

To get to that reality, however, you have to go beyond the image of the Deity. The image itself is the true gateway to the transcendental, formless Absolute, so when you go beyond the image you begin to understand the real nature of the Deity, which is omnipresent, omniscient, omnipotent, beyond description, beyond any limitations whatsoever. It is necessary, however, for human beings to start off with some *form*, something they can relate to, because it is not possible to visualize a boundless ocean of reality! Not even an angel, archangel or one of the Elohīm can visualize that which is absolute.

To summarize, the faculty of imagination or visualization is nature-born within everyone and what we visualize is what we become. You can visualize any kind of situation for yourself in material life, or you can choose the spiritual way, the Ninth Gate, *Visualizing the Real*. The intermediary stage is visualizing the Divine Form, the form of the Christ, the Buddha, Kṛṣṇa, Rama or one of the great Saints or Avatāras. Then, you go beyond that to the original Reality; that is, you go beyond the objectified forms of Reality to the unmanifest, unconditioned form of Reality, the true Reality. That form or image of a deity will take you halfway there, but at a certain point you have to drop it and allow the Infinitude, the Eternal Life, to come on its own. When the image dissolves and the Gate opens by itself, you merge into the Ocean of Absolute Reality.

This is why the Zen Teachers say, "If you see the Buddha, kill him!" They understand this principle and are of course speaking from the spiritual perspective. It doesn't mean that if you see a Buddha you should shoot him. No, if you see the image of the Buddha inside you (because you have come to that stage where you can identify and locate the Buddha Consciousness within), then destroy it, that is, *let it go*. Then you can merge into the real Buddha, which is the Transcendental Absolute, the unimaginable splendour of Reality. If you are still seeing the Buddha it limits you to that particular experience.

The Way of Visualizing the Real is a most amazing path, because it uses a natural faculty which everybody has. All of the Nine Ways are very natural, based on the composition of the Cosmos and of the human being. There is nothing external that has to be introduced, nothing artificially created or produced. They just use what a human being is and what the Cosmos is to enable the human being to reach Enlightenment.

1

☿
♀

MERCURY

THE MAGUS OF POWER

TRANSPARENT INTELLIGENCE

The Master of circumstances, Initiative Power,
Determination, Will

BETH
2
HOUSE

Tarot Key 1—The Magus of Power

A Dynamic, Positive Attitude to Life and the Mastery of All Circumstances

We mentioned the power of symbols, that they have an impact on your Feminine Mind (subconscious mind), and we described the creative process of *what you see, you become*, which works itself out in your physical life in the same way that thoughtforms in the Divine Mind work out into physical manifestation as the Physical Universe. As an example of the power of symbols, I have chosen Tarot Key 1, *The Magus of Power*, because it has two major themes that have practicality in daily life: a dynamic, positive attitude to life and the mastery of all circumstances.

If you feel your life is not dynamic or positive or if you are one of those chaotic persons who do not know what they are doing from day to day or from hour to hour, then this symbol can completely revolutionize your whole existence. Many people are unhappy; they are not satisfied with what they are doing or they feel that nothing in life is satisfying. When dissatisfied, of course, people blame somebody or something else as the cause of it—which it isn't. No matter who your partner is, what your job is, what the weather is or what the government is, you will never be satisfied until you have the energy of the Magus of Power—the *Magician*—working inside you; in fact, until you *become* the Magus of Power. [16]

---

[16] A colour version of Tarot Key 1 can be downloaded from www.planetary-transformation.org/key1.

Nowadays, there are many courses on positive thinking and how to deal with people and situations, but the problem is that they are all on the mind level and there is no essential inner change. You can think positively but if the inner mind, the inner being, remains negative, all you are doing is creating an artificial situation whereby you are positive. But if you work with this Tarot Key, that is, if you colour it in, put it in a place where you can see it often in your day-to-day life and visualize the image in formal meditation sessions, you will actually become dynamic and positive and at the same time you will master all circumstances in your life. You won't have to convince yourself or try to work it out in your mind; you *will be* positive, dynamic and the master of your life. Once you become the Magician, no situation will bring you down, none of the external tragedies in life will diminish your ability to be positive and to handle all situations with mastery and skill.

It is important to distinguish between the way colour is used in the Tarot Keys and the way it is used in society. In New Age bookshops nowadays, you will find many different sets of Tarot Keys—everything from Aboriginal cards to angel cards to fairy cards—created by imaginative artists who want to make an impression or impact on people. These artists don't know the science behind the Tarot, how to put colours and shapes together to produce particular effects, because they have no esoteric understanding of what Tarot Keys are. In actuality, the Tarot Keys are precise, scientifically developed symbols based on the harmony of colour, shape and form and their relations in the Inner Worlds. To compose symbols like the Tarot Keys, which speak directly to the inner mind, you have to understand the Science of Symbols and know how colours and shapes affect people.

The Masters of ancient Egypt first devised the Tarot and the first Keys were painted on temple walls and pillars. They depicted certain god and goddess figures, and the Masters knew exactly what each figure meant and how the worshippers would be influenced by it. After the Egyptian civilization fell, some Initiates decided to revive the Tarot in the Middle East, using European symbols rather than Egyptian symbols, which no one would have understood. For instance, we can easily identify with a Magician but not one of the animal-headed gods of the Egyptians.

I will briefly explain the composition of Tarot Key 1 so that you understand how it is put together to produce the effect of dynamic positivity and to give you a sense of mastery, of being in control of your life. When the first Master thought how to represent these qualities, he started by looking inside and visualizing what he wanted to bring forth and then considering which physical colours would give these particular qualities based on the Science of Colour and Form. To get the impact of a dynamic and positive attitude, therefore, he used the colour vibrations that correspond to those qualities as the main colours of Key 1: red and yellow; dynamic and positive.

In the Tarot Key, the Magician is standing in a garden, which shows that there is some living process involved, since a garden always represents life and growth. This means that the Magician is working with living substances, with a *living* reality. In front of the Magician is a table on which are the tools that the Magician uses: the *spear*, which represents the element Fire; the *cup*, which represents the element Water; the *sword*, which represents the element Air; and the *coin*, which represents the element Earth. This tells us that the Magician works with the elements that constitute Creation (the Physical, Astral, Mental and Causal Worlds), the elements out of which everything is made, and he controls, guides and formulates them according to his will, to shape his own destiny—the *master of all circumstances*.

Notice the attitude of the Magician. He is pointing his finger downwards towards the four elements, which means that he is focusing on life, on the circumstances he is in. His mind is sharply focused and one hundred per cent in the moment. When you visualize this picture in your mind, your inner psychic mechanism, your Feminine Mind, tries to imitate the Magician. So you will become more focused, more concentrated in the moment and better able to handle your day-to-day circumstances. This means that when you are in a situation you don't know how to handle, you will see the problem or the situation clearly, without your mind wobbling all over the place, so you will see the solution immediately.

Notice, also, that there are two kinds of flowers in the Tarot Key: roses and lilies. In Christianity, the rose is an important symbol, especially the rose and the cross, and to the ancient Jews, the white lily of the valley was an important symbol. In the East, the lotus flower is important, symbolizing the mysteries of life and transcendental awareness. But because the Tarot is a Western system, the Jewish lily and the Christian rose are used.

The red *roses* represent intense desire, the emotional quality needed to transform one's life; whatever you intensely desire or emotionally propel will become manifest. This shows that whatever the Magician desires to become, to create or to change will become manifest. The four *lilies* represent the four functions of the mind. This means that the Magician uses memory and logic, the lowest functions of the mind; the causal mind, which is meta-logical, the ability to see abstract principles instantaneously; and the Cosmic Mind, with its infinitely greater powers. In other words, the Magician uses the mental faculty to shape the elements that constitute a particular situation according to what he desires.

The two-ended *wand* in the Magician's hand represents Light. This shows that the Magician brings the Light down through himself and directs it into his magical work. It is through the power of Light that life becomes dynamic and positive and all circumstances are mastered and controlled. The *power* of the Light within is represented by the Magician's *white inner garment*. A master Magician works with the Light-force so that his or her understanding and intelligence are far superior to those of a normal person. And the *infinity symbol* above the Magician's head shows that his Crown Cakra is activated by the Light and is channelling the Divine Energy (Śakti or Shekinah) into his whole being.

The *brown table* represents the material world. Brown always symbolizes physical objects because it is a mixture of colours. And the *serpent* around the Magician's waist shows that he lives in a timeless condition, which means that although he is working in time and space, in the here and now, he is nevertheless enclosed in the sensation of eternal beingness.

Visualizing Yourself as the Magician

First, focus your attention in the here and now, which is the point of creativity because it is in the moment that things are what they are, and it is in the moment that change can happen. Look at a coloured copy of Tarot Key 1 for a few minutes, holding it slightly above eye level. Then, close your eyes and visualize, in full colour, the four objects on the table that symbolize the elements; the roses that represent the inner desire nature; and the lilies that symbolize the knowledge field of the mind. Lastly, visualize yourself standing like the Magician.

About This Technique

To apply this in your daily life, suppose you have a problem at work. Spend half an hour or so visualizing yourself as the Magician and allowing the Light to come through. This tells your inner mind that you want to be like the Magician. Focus on being in the moment, not on the problem, aligning yourself with the immediate reality of the moment. Then, recall your problem for an instant, and in that instant the all-knowing energy-field of the Light will reshuffle the elements of the situation and reveal to you what the cause of the problem is, so that you can automatically start putting it right.

*****

The beauty of this system is that it is so natural. Even if you find it difficult to concentrate and visualize the Tarot Key, it will still work for you if you have it somewhere in your house and look at it while you are washing the dishes or doing something around the house. Your Feminine Mind works in symbols and understands symbols perfectly. You simply present that symbol and the Feminine Mind will say, "Gosh, he wants to be positive; so let's make him positive," and then it will automatically start working. It's a very easy path.

*****

You don't have to sit crossed-legged or assume any special position, just look at the Tarot Key. When you mentally visualize the image, the colours will first register in your mind (not your brain). Each colour has a certain rate of vibration and the combination of colours is a whole set of vibrations, and the vibrations have to go from your mental body to your physical brain. Once that happens, the physical brain speeds up according to the impulses given by the particular colour vibrations. This is how your transformation begins.

Those in the healing field and the field of alternative medicine know that the colours in this Tarot Key are extraordinarily good for giving physical energy and dynamism. Red is good for physical strength and energy. Yellow sharpens the mind, making it bright and clear. And green is good for vitality, as well as being healing and harmonious, because it is the colour of life—Nature is green. This Key also has a bit of blue, which gives the feminine, receptive qualities of water, so it has a colour combination scientifically designed to make you a more perfect and healthy human being.

*****

The next Tarot Key in the Tarot System, Tarot Key 2, is predominantly blue, the complete reverse of Tarot Key 1. Key 1 will create activity and dynamism inside you, but if you are overactive and want to pacify and calm yourself down, then you would use the blue vibration of Tarot Key 2 to become passive. Key 2 will reverse the outgoing dynamic energies and you will become absorbed in your inner world and become quiet. But if you use it too much, that quietness makes you ineffective and you can become depressed or have what they call "the blues". Similarly, if you use too much red you can become violent and agitated; if you use too much yellow you become an intellectual who has no heart. If a colour is overused it can produce the opposite effect to that intended.

So there are two things to note: to use the right colour for the right purpose and to use colours in the right proportion. Any colour will be destructive if it is overused, and if you don't have a particular colour vibration inside you, you will be prone to disease or sickness. In other words, you can analyse a person's state of health by what colours they have or don't have inside them. People who have too much blue vibration inside them are generally weak, and unhealthy people normally have no green vibration in them. When you are a totally integrated person, all the seven colours are pulsating inside you in an even and stable way. So ill health can be caused by the lack of a particular colour or too much of a particular colour. That is a whole science in itself.

*****

Each Tarot Key has been precisely and scientifically devised and the symbols, colours and all the elements are there for particular reasons. Therefore, they must not be changed. That is why you have to be careful when choosing Tarot cards. How the world understands the use of colour is sometimes correct and sometimes not. Many cards you see nowadays are based on imagination, on colours and symbols somebody thinks are nice.

*****

There are those who try to heal people with pendulums or crystals or complicated colour arrangements, when all that is needed is to give them the right Tarot Keys. You don't need any other gadgets. That's because the colours you see are not just colours but *energy-fields*. When you look at a colour, the colour itself doesn't do anything to you; it only reminds your inner consciousness, your Feminine Mind, that you want to work with that energy. Your Feminine Mind, being feminine and receptive, then connects you to that colour *internally*, giving you a sense of the energy-field behind the colour. Then you can sense the blueness or the redness or the greenness and feel the specific vibration of the colour. Outwardly, the Tarot Key looks like a picture, but your inner mind sees the real dynamic energy-field behind the picture.

BONDAGE AND LIBERATION

The Nine Paths to Enlightenment are open to all human beings, regardless of race, creed or nationality. At this critical juncture in the history of our planet, with the coming of the New Energy of the Planetary Avatāra, it is essential that as many people as possible prepare themselves *spiritually* for the coming changes. The need for Enlightenment, however, existed long before the present age and will continue as long as Humanity remains in Ignorance. It is timeless because it is rooted in the human existential condition, which is the state of Bondage. So the Nine Paths to Enlightenment are not only the means we need to help transform the planet today but also the gateways to personal Liberation for all time.

Eastern religions talk about Bondage and Liberation, but very few people understand what they are, thinking that they are theories or philosophies about reality. They are not theories, however, but vital facts that you have to understand, because you are in the state of Bondage. If you are in a prison in chains you understand what bondage is; and if somebody frees you, then you know what liberation is. But before you can be *truly liberated* you must know what Bondage is, because only then can you start working intelligently toward your Liberation. So

I'll tell you what it is:

Bondage is compulsive and compulsory reincarnation into this world by Cosmic Law.

Notice: Bondage is *compulsive* and *compulsory* reincarnation—compulsory because you are required by the Law of Karma to do it, and compulsive because you yourself want to do it. So that's the state of Bondage. Human beings are forced to incarnate and they can do nothing about it, and they want to incarnate because it's a kind of disease in their consciousness. Have you ever thought why you have to come back here all the time? Of course, you may come back because you want to be the emperor of Rome or because there are so many wonderful things here, but what you don't know is that the Inner Worlds are a billion times better than this world! The problem is, you can't choose them because of the Cosmic Law.

The question is: why do you have to come back? This is important because if you understand the answer to this question you will liberate yourself in this lifetime.

The Cycle of Reincarnation

Past Impressions (Vāsanās or Saṁskāras) are stored in the subconscious mind.

First of all you have to know that the mind has several regions—subconscious, self-conscious and superconscious—and that the subconscious mind is the Female Mind, the Mother Principle. From the esoteric or theosophical point of view, your subconscious mind is what we call the astral body or the astral self, and the Planetary

Subconscious Mind is what we call the Astral World, or the Astral Light that surrounds and permeates the whole planet.

Now, past impressions are stored in the subconscious mind. This is the basis of the whole cycle of Reincarnation.

In Sanskrit[17], *past impressions* are called Vāsanās or Saṁskāras, which mean "hidden influences", "subtle energy-fields" or "subtle states that exert influence". These past impressions have been created since the beginning of time, that is to say, from the time Humanity descended from the Nirvanic dimensions to the Buddhic dimensions and then to the causal, mental, astral and finally the physical dimensions. All your impressions are stored in your subconscious mind, which you could say is your immediate connection to this physical world, and it is the same with the planet: all the impressions and activities of Humanity and of the Angelic Kingdom and the Animal, Plant and Mineral Kingdoms are stored in the Planetary Subconscious Mind (the Astral World), and they influence planetary life. This is a basic fact of Nature; you cannot get away from it no matter what philosophy you follow.

So, past impressions are stored in your subconscious mind, which in itself is just a fact. The question is, how do you deal with them, or what actually happens to you as a result of these impressions?

And this is where the problem lies:

THESE IMPRESSIONS NEED TO BE WORKED OUT BY THE CREATIVE POWER OF YOUR SUBCONSCIOUS MIND, THE FEMALE MIND, THE MOTHER PRINCIPLE.

.

[17] The Sanskrit language is amazing. It has thousands of words that refer to esoteric or spiritual knowledge. There's no other language in the world that can come near it in terms of spiritual terminology, no other language that has as many words describing the hidden, invisible realities.

The Law of the Female Mind, the subconscious mind, is that once something has been put into the subconscious mind, she has to by Cosmic Law reproduce it, or bring it into manifestation in the physical world. This is a great esoteric secret, and it is how magic and supernatural powers work. If we extend this to the planetary level: whatever has been put into the subconscious mind of the planet over the thousands of years of human activity has to be brought into manifestation. The result? Earthquakes, fires, tribulations, wars, political unrest—all the problems you see in the world today. What we put in, we get out.

In other words, what we've been putting into the subconscious mind of our planet are the 'rewards' we are reaping now. We have endless wars and endless troubles simply because that is what we programmed the Planetary Subconscious Mind to do. While there are billions of people constantly putting out negative energy, the planet will be as crazy as it is. It's the Law. It's only we who can stop it: by reprogramming the Planetary Subconscious Mind, by being intelligent for a change, by understanding the laws of Nature and then working *with* those laws.

On the individual level, the impressions that you put into your subconscious mind in the past have to be worked out on the physical level, and therefore you are forced to reincarnate. On a larger scale, because of the impressions we have put into the subconscious mind of the planet, Humanity is forced to reincarnate. That's why there are always billions of people struggling to reincarnate. Why would people want to be born in this mess? Because they are forced to; because in previous times they put the wrong impressions into the planetary mind structure, which by Cosmic Law has to work them out in the physical dimension. So the billions of humans are forced into incarnation to bring that about.

This means the wars will go on, the troubles will go on and the misery of life will go on as it has since long before Buddha, who said that life is misery. And why is life misery? Because we (the intelligent species we are!) *create* misery. We are always feeding the Planetary Subconscious Mind with negativity and she has to bring it about. It's self-perpetuating.

We mentioned before that no one is an island; we all influence each other. If there is violence in a family, it gets passed on to the children, who pass on the violent behaviour pattern to their children, and so it goes life after life, incarnation after incarnation. But, it could also work for the good. One generation could be good and hand over goodness to the next generation. The Law is the same, except we are not doing the right thing. This is where free will comes in. You have to be responsible for yourself, families have to be responsible for themselves, groups have to be responsible for themselves, countries have to be responsible for themselves.

At this stage, therefore, the past impressions have to be worked out, so you are forced to reincarnate and the violence in society keeps going on, with one generation giving it to the next. Don't worry, though, there is an end to this. I have to tell you all the stages of Liberation right from the beginning. You won't work for Liberation unless you understand that you are in Bondage. Then you will want to be Free, and not just keep incarnating all the time.

Now, here's the next part of the story:

AS YOU ARE WORKING OUT YOUR KARMAS IN THIS LIFETIME YOU ARE CREATING FURTHER IMPRESSIONS (VĀSANĀS) WHICH HAVE TO BE WORKED OUT IN THE NEXT LIFE.

That's what I call being in a big stew. And that's why we don't have so many Buddhas on this planet and why the violence keeps going on generation after generation.

So from previous lifetimes you have impressions in your subconscious mind that you are busily working out. Those are the karmas which come to you. All the things that happen to you in your lifetime—good bad and indifferent—are simply the working out of karmas from the past. But—and this is a big but—at the same time you are creating new impressions. Every time you have a fight with somebody, every time you do something wrong to somebody, every time you do good to somebody, every time you do anything, you put further impressions in your subconscious mind—and she is quite happy knowing that she will be busy again in your next life!

Whatever we do always has a past cause. If you belong to a fundamentalist religion, it means that you belonged to that religion previously and you reincarnated and are carrying on with that same impression now. On the other hand, if you belong to an esoteric school, it means that in a previous time you belonged to an esoteric school and learned some wisdom and understanding and now your Soul brings you back to an esoteric school where you can further your knowledge. *Nothing* is accidental; nothing is haphazard. Everything is done one hundred percent by law. Whatever you experience today, both bad and good, is because of your past, and whatever you do now is also seeding your future. So is there an end to it? How do we stop it? The answer lies in the way the Cosmos works:

FOR YOUR SOUL TO BE FREE, YOU MUST NEUTRALIZE THE NEGATIVE IMPRESSIONS IN YOUR SUBCONSCIOUS MIND AND REPLACE THEM WITH POSITIVE IMPRESSIONS AND TRANSCENDING IMPRESSIONS.

This is why all the religions, even if they have no esoteric knowledge, stress the idea that you have to be virtuous, and why they make rules about not killing, not stealing, and so on. Because human beings tend to generate negative impressions, every religion creates dos and don'ts for its followers and all the great Teachers have told people what to do and not do. But most people don't understand why those dos and don'ts were given to them because they were never given the esoteric science behind the rules. The science behind them is: if your subconscious mind contains negative impressions, it's going to keep reproducing them in your life—lifetime after lifetime. In other words, you have to get the negative energies out of your subconscious mind, *but not by continually thinking about them.* This is a wrong technique that psychology uses nowadays, always focusing on past miseries and other negative experiences.

The right technique involves replacing the negative impressions in your subconscious mind by putting in positive impressions *and* transcending impressions. By *transcending impressions* we mean impressions that will convince your Female Mind (subconscious mind) to work for your Liberation, for transcending the physical dimension, transcending your personality; impressions that will elevate you and make you want to move upwards into the higher dimensions; impressions that tell your subconscious mind you want to attain higher states of consciousness, the state of Enlightenment, Union with God. If the subconscious mind only receives impressions of *this* lifetime and *this* world, she will produce incarnation into this world and bring about other lifetimes similar to this one because she has not been given any other instructions—and nothing changes.

The key is to understand the law that every human being is born with negative impressions which are brought with them from their own subconscious mind and play out in their lifetime, and which have to be replaced with impressions that are not only positive but also transcend this dimension altogether. To achieve this, you have to develop certain qualities. This is not new; right from the time of Hermes Trismegistus, the great Avatāra of ancient Egypt, the Masters have always taught that if you want to go on the Spiritual Path you have to develop certain qualities or virtues.

(1) Peace of Mind

The first quality you have to develop is *peace of mind*, because it will bring the subconscious mind into a positive state. If your mind is peaceful, then that peace becomes an impression in your subconscious mind, which will start working on the project that you want peace and tranquillity from all the problems and troubles in your life. Peace of mind is the number-one quality, and not just because Buddha said it was, but because it will work on your subconscious mind in a positive, healthy way and then your subconscious mind will start working positively towards your Liberation.

So you have to work on getting peace of mind through various meditation and breathing techniques that help you have a balanced state of mind, and be conscious that you have to have peace of mind and try to live it on a daily basis. I know that acquiring this quality is not easy; it's not something you can do in half an hour. But if you understand that you need it to reprogramme your subconscious mind and attain Liberation in this lifetime, if you understand the science behind it, then you will keep it in mind. For instance, after you've had an argument with somebody and you realize that you have lost your peace of mind, you will talk to that person and try to work things out in order to get back to your level of peace of mind.

(2) *Contentment in Your Life*

Like the other qualities, *contentment in your life* is difficult to achieve when you first start but becomes easier later on, once your subconscious mind has been reprogrammed. *Contentment in your life* means that you are happy with where you are at and what you are doing and how you are, without wanting to be something else. One of the main causes of disturbance in human life is that people always want more: if you have one car you want to have two; if you have two cars you want to have a boat; if you have a boat you want to have a helicopter. The endless greed of wanting more and more shows that you are not happy with your life. And if you are not happy, then what? You put into your subconscious mind that state of *discontent* and are always tense and nervous, and nothing will satisfy you, nothing will make you happy.

Remember, this is not something you can achieve straight away but something you have to work towards, realizing that it is better to be happy with your circumstances than working seventy-two hours a week to become something else. This usually requires great effort and sometimes wrong ways of working—exploiting people or Nature or driving yourself to a nervous breakdown—and it always produces a lot of stress, which goes into the subconscious mind, which produces further stress, even an incarnation full of stress. Hospitals are full of people who suffer from stress simply because they are not content with their lives.

As you can see, we're talking about your whole life pattern, your whole life path, not just one little aspect. So you have to work on having peace of mind: try to keep yourself in balance as much as you can and re-establish it when you lose that balance; and contentment in your life: be content in yourself, in a simple lifestyle, and be happy to be focusing on the *inner realities*, the important things of life.

(3) Meditation

The next thing you need is Meditation. We have said much about Meditation in this book and in other books[18], so here we will only point out that, generally speaking, there are two kinds of meditation techniques: those which take you beyond the personality level to the state of being and those which put positive impressions in your subconscious mind and take you to the state of becoming something positive. In other words, Meditation not only produces *positive* impressions that neutralize the negative impressions in your subconscious mind but also *transcending* impressions that help you attain states of Higher Consciousness.

(4) Being in Contact with a Wise Person—a Guru or Master

Being in contact with a Wise Person—a Guru or Master, somebody who understands the esoteric laws of life—is in a way the most important factor because it's from this that everything else follows. If you are in contact with somebody who is Wise, then you are bound to pick up some Wisdom, Understanding and Knowledge from that person. That's why every tradition all over the world stresses that you should "seek yourself a Master", "seek yourself a Guru".

In the 1960s, 70s and 80s there was an anti-Guru sentiment among the so-called liberated new agers (who never really became liberated), and there were many intellectuals who said that they didn't need a Guru or a Master, they knew it all themselves. Well, they didn't; they tried all kinds of things and usually got themselves into a lot of trouble. A Wise Person is needed in your life for the simple reason that they put you on the right track and *keep* you on the right track. Otherwise,

---

[18] See my books *The Art of Meditation* (2nd ed., 2007), *Heavens & Hells of the Mind* (2007), *Planetary Transformation* (2010), and other titles listed in the publisher's catalogue and Web site.

you get lost in intellectualism—you read up this philosophy and that, this theology and that, and you go to this school and that; your mind gets filled up with all kinds of information and you think that you know how to liberate yourself on your own. There's a big difference between being intellectual and really being liberated, so having a Wise Person in your life is all-important.

(5) Intense Desire for Liberation

The last quality you must have is an intense desire for Liberation. Most people don't understand how important this is. In order to attain Freedom in this lifetime, you have to really want it. There's a story in the sacred literature of India about a Guru and a young disciple who were walking along a riverbank, when the disciple asked the Guru how he could attain Liberation. The Guru grabbed the disciple by the hair and pushed his head under the water, and didn't let him go until he was just about out of air. "What did you do that for?" asked the disciple. "Well," the Guru said, "when you desire Liberation as much as you desired the air, you will get Liberation." Some Gurus have strange ways of teaching.

If you are wishy-washy about liberating yourself, you will never get there. You can attain Freedom *in this lifetime*, if you understand the principles we have described, develop the aforementioned qualities, and have a strong desire for it. Historically, very few people attained Liberation because their desire wasn't strong enough, and that is a big part of why people fail nowadays. They give some attention to Liberation every now and then but most of the time they're too busy doing worldly things, or they decide to start meditating just before they die, when it's too late. The whole idea is that your whole life has to be reformed and reorganized toward your goal.

So unless you have an intense desire for Liberation, you won't succeed. Again, this is not a rule invented by a Guru or a philosophy. It's a law of Life, a law of Nature. So you have to ask yourself, do you really want Liberation (or God-Realization, Self-Realization, Nirvāṇa, Peace, whatever you want to call it)? Because if you do, then a magic thing happens: that strong desire will start working in your subconscious mind, and she will start putting energies and powers inside you and give you the willpower you need to succeed.

And that brings us to the final result: Liberation itself.

Liberation manifests as experiences of Higher Consciousness.

Intellectuals think that being clever is liberation. They know what the Vedanta philosophy is, what the Buddhist philosophy is, what the Christian theology is, and they think they are enlightened. But that has nothing to do with Enlightenment. You can be clever and bright—and there are many bright minds in all fields—but that is not Liberation. Liberation manifests as experiences of Higher Consciousness. In other words, you know that you are on the way to Liberation when you begin to have transcendental visions or experiences, transcendental touches, sensitivity to the Inner Worlds, sensitivity to the presence of the Deity, identification with the Spirit. These are signs that you are on the way to Liberation; not whether you are clever or not. This is important because many Zen practitioners get lost in high-frequency intellectualism, which has nothing to do with Liberation. Liberation is experiencing higher states of consciousness, full stop. It's not a mind game.

And this is the end of the story:

THEN THE PAST IMPRESSIONS (VĀSANĀS) IN YOUR
SUBCONSCIOUS MIND BECOME NEUTRALIZED AND
THERE IS NO MORE COMPULSORY REINCARNATION.

This is the final knowledge on this subject: Liberation manifests
as experiences of Higher Consciousness and as you experience those
higher states, the past impressions (Vāsanās) in your subconscious
mind become neutralized. The very power and high frequency of the
higher states of consciousness neutralize and obliterate the Vāsanās,
and because they are neutralized there are no more *causes for reincarnation*,
no more forces you have to work out by coming into physical
being. It's as simple as that.

This means that you can be liberated at any age. Ramana Maharishi
was fourteen, I attained Liberation at the age of nineteen, and
some get it in middle age or later. But Liberation doesn't mean that
you drop your physical body and quit the world. No, a person who is
liberated in their lifetime carries on in the physical body doing all the
things they were meant to do from previous lifetimes; for example,
I've been a Teacher in India for several lifetimes. So if you are liberated
you follow on with what your Soul set out to do in this lifetime. The
only difference is that you are not bound by anything in your lifetime;
you simply do your duty, whatever that may be. But even while you're
doing things you are Free because there are no new patterns put in
your subconscious mind. When you die, therefore, there are no forces
to bring you back into incarnation. You go wherever you want in the
Inner Worlds; you are a Free Person. Of course, you can also choose to
come back as a Teacher in order to help Humanity. You have a choice
to do whatever you like, and that's true Freedom.

In Sanskrit, becoming liberated while in the physical body is referred to as JĪVAN-MUKTI, but there is another way to become liberated, called VIDEHĀ-MUKTI, in which you are liberated in the after-death condition. How this works is, suppose you have started the process of becoming liberated in this lifetime and have done a lot of meditation and much work towards it but haven't reached the state of Enlightenment by the time you die. When you drop your physical body and are in your astral body in the Astral World, your subconscious mind keeps working on the project (because your astral body is your subconscious mind and the Astral World is the subconscious mind of the planet).

Remember, your subconscious mind has to work on whatever programme has been put in, so she carries on working on that project in the inner dimensions until you attain Liberation. It's therefore possible to be liberated after you die, provided you have done a sufficient amount of work in this lifetime and motivated your inner consciousness to carry on with the same pattern in the after-death condition. So if you have set into motion positive energy-fields to neutralize the negative energies in your subconscious mind and have also put in transcending energies, then she will work with the same energies in the after-death condition, leading you from the higher Astral World to the lower Mental World to the higher Mental World (the Causal World) and then to the Buddhic World. Then you are liberated in the same cycle of *this* lifetime, and you don't have to reincarnate. You are Free—forever.

GLOSSARY

The following are excerpts from *Heavens & Hells of the Mind*, Volume 4: *Lexicon of the Wisdom Language*, by the author.

ADVAITA, ĀDVAITA
Sanskrit: "Not two". Non-duality, Oneness, Unity. The All-Oneness.

ĀKĀŚA
Sanskrit: Space. Heaven. The All-Light of Reality. Space in its totality as the physical body of God. "Space" does not mean some kind of emptiness in which particles of matter float. ĀKĀŚA does not mean there is "nothing there"; on the contrary, ĀKĀŚA means that *all* is there—total Fullness. To the ancients, the word *Heaven* (Space) did not mean just the physical sky, but the inner, invisible worlds and spaces as well.

ANĀHATA-NĀDA
Sanskrit: "The Unproduced Sound", meaning "not produced by external means", heard in the Heart Centre.

ĀNANDA
Sanskrit: Bliss, Joy, Happiness, Ecstasy. The highest pleasure or enjoyment. Bliss is the very nature of Spirit (the Monad), and of You as a Soul.

Aquarian Age
As our Solar Logos (the Sun) moves about in space it comes under the influence of each sign of the Zodiac for approximately 2,150 years. Currently the Piscean Age is ending and the

Aquarian radiations are beginning to be felt throughout our Solar System, changing, renewing, re-creating all things. This is why this New Age is often called the *Aquarian Age*. The ending of an Age and the beginning of a New Age is always *traumatic* for Humanity.

ARMAGEDDON

Hebrew: "Battlefield". From the Hebrew HARMEGIDDON (HAR, "mountain", and MEGIDDON, "the Valley of Megiddo"). In ancient Palestine there was a great battle fought in a mountain district called Megiddo, in Northern Palestine. In spiritual literature, the word ARMAGEDDON refers to the Battle between the personality and the Soul—the Spiritual Crisis.

ASCENSION

Latin: In the symbolism of the New Testament, *Ascension* is the Union of body, mind and Soul with God. It is the entry into NIRVĀṆA, the Kingdom of God.

ĀŚRAMA

Sanskrit: Stages of development in life. Also, a hermitage, a monastery or spiritual centre. In the West we call them the *Mystery Schools*. The Work of the Mystery Schools and ĀŚRAMAs is the expansion of Consciousness, alignment with one's own Higher Self, Spiritual Illumination, and service toward the Group Soul and the world, under the guidance of the Guru, the Hierophant, the Spiritual Master.

Astral Body

A form or vehicle made up of astral matter, existing on the Astral Plane. Every single entity—a human being, a bird, a tree, an animal—has an astral body. The astral body is a luminous form which interpenetrates the physical form. It is the more real part of your nature, for the physical form is only an extension of this luminous body. In Sanskrit it is called SŪKṢMA-ŚARĪRA (subtle body) and KĀMA-RŪPA (desire-body). Your astral body is your *dream-body*, in which you dream. In modern terminology it is known as your *subconscious mind*.

Astral Plane

"The starry realm". The sixth of the seven great Planes of Being. The Astral Plane is the world of the dead, where people go after they die. In the East it is known as KĀMA-LOKA, "the realm of desires". It is the realm of emotion and feelings, of psychic energies and forces, of the *subconscious mind*. The seven astral subplanes, or seven states of astral matter, correspond to the various heavens, hells and purgatories of the world religions.

Astrologos, Astrologia

Greek: "The science of the stars". The study of cosmic rays, energies and influences. The study of the motions of the planets in relationship to our Sun and how they affect Humanity collectively and individually. The science of the influence of the subtle radiations of the heavenly bodies (planets and stars) upon our Earth and upon Man. Hence the English word *astrology*. Astrology has been abused by the ignorant, the uninitiated, the superstitious. But the true science of astrology is a fact, and is just as real as chemistry or biology.

Astronomy

The science of the *material universe* beyond Earth's atmosphere.

Atlantis

Atlantean civilization extended over a vast area encompassing parts of the Atlantic Ocean, North America and Europe. Ancient legends and mythologies refer to that once-glorious civilization, but it was too long ago for people to remember accurately. What happened in Atlantis was not merely physical, but encompassed the astral dimensions as well.

Ātmā, Ātma, Ātman

Sanskrit: The Life-Breath of God the Absolute. The Self-Luminous Being, the Light of the Eternal, the Bright Eternal Self, the Spiritual Self, the Universal Spirit or Self within All. Ātman is the Universal Divine I AM, of which Man is a part. It is the Innermost Spirit in Man, the true Man dwelling on the Nirvāṇic Plane, also known as Puruṣa (the Cosmic Man). Ātman is the One Divine Self in the human species, the Universal Principle that gives the sensation of "Selfhood" to the Divine in Man.

Avatāra

Sanskrit: A Divine Incarnation. One who has descended from the Light Realms. From Ava (down) and Tāra (to pass, to go), or Ava-Trī (to come down, to descend). There are Cosmic Avatāras, Solar-Systemic Avatāras, Planetary Avatāras and Human Avatāras— those who appear to Humanity and the Devas for the purpose of speeding up their evolution and aiding the Divinization of the planet. An Avatāra incarnates for a specific purpose. (The corrupted anglicized form is *Avatar*.)

Bhajan

Sanskrit: Inner worship. Heart chant. Deeply devotional, meditative, contemplative, invocative singing and chanting.

BODHISATTVA

Sanskrit: "One whose very essence is Wisdom and Love". From BODHI (Love-Wisdom) and SATTVA (essence, being, quality). An enlightened Seer or Sage. A NIRMĀNAKĀYA whose essence is Love-Wisdom. An Enlightened Being who does not merge into Nirvāṇa but remains on the Buddhic and Causal Planes. A Buddha who sacrifices his or her own Enlightenment for the welfare of Mankind.

BUDDHA

Sanskrit: "Inwardly wide awake". One who is awake within himself. From BUDH, "to blossom, to bloom, to wake up, to know". This does not mean someone who is awake on the Physical Plane in the physical body. It means One who has awakened from the Sleep of Ignorance, who is awake on a very high plane of our Solar System, who is in a very high state of Consciousness.

Buddhic Plane

The fourth of the seven great Planes of Being. The Buddhic Plane has been called the *Realm of Unities* or the *Intuitional World*. It is a formless Light World characterized by Divine Unity, Love and Wisdom. The state of BUDDHI is Unitive Consciousness, Transcendental Consciousness or Pure Consciousness, wherein the Mystic experiences Oneness with the Universe and with God. The Sūfī Mystics called this realm 'ĀLAM-I-MALAKŪT, "the World of the Kingdom" (the Kingdom of God). In Christianity it is known as the *Christ Realm* or *Paradise*. In Sanskrit, MAHAH-LOKA. On this plane you are already Liberated.

CAKRA

Sanskrit: A circle, a wheel, a sphere, an orb, a revolving disk, a whirlpool of energy, a rotating centre, a wheel of fire. The term can refer to an atom, a planet, a solar system, a galaxy, a planetary vortex, or an Energy Centre in a human being. The Solar System is a large CAKRA, and each of the planets is a CAKRA within the Solar System. In a human being, the CAKRAs are subtle Energy Centres in the etheric, astral, mental and causal bodies.

Causal Body

The causal body (KĀRAṆA-ŚARĪRA in Sanskrit) is made up of matter of the three highest subplanes of the Mental Plane—the ARŪPA or formless levels. This is your Higher MANAS or Abstract Mind. Your causal body is the lowest part of your imperishable Individuality (ĀTMA-BUDDHI-MANAS), beyond your personality complex. Your Reincarnating Ego (JĪVA, you as a Human Soul) dwells in your causal body. Your karmas are stored up in your causal body, thus giving you the continuity of existence, life after life.

Causal World

The three higher subplanes of the Mental Plane, which are formless (ARŪPA). Also known as the *Archetypal World*. The Causal Worlds are realms of formless Ideas and Archetypes, which are the "cause" of all that manifests in the Three Worlds. (Note that the Causal Worlds are formless from *our* point of view.)

Channelling

From the Latin CANAL: "A waterway". Used nowadays to mean *mediumship*—receiving messages from the dead or from discarnate entities. Usually the medium speaks from her or his own subconscious mind. In rarer cases, an outside entity temporarily possesses the medium, psychic or sensitive and gives messages. Sometimes the term refers to the "channelling" of one's own Soul Wisdom, which has no relation to mediumship.

Christ

From the Latin KRISTUS, which came from the Greek CHRISTOS, which meant "the Anointed One, the Sacred One, the Holy One", one who has attained the grade of Supreme Hierophant of the Mysteries, after the custom in the Greek Mystery Schools of anointing an Initiate with precious oils and perfumes after he or she had passed all the tests and triumphed, or risen to Higher Consciousness. The Christ is threefold:

- Christ is the Great Being called MAITREYA, who is the Heart of our Spiritual Hierarchy (the Communion of the Saints of all religions).

- Christ is also the Spirit-Spark-Atom in your Heart which responds to the Call from the Christ of the Spiritual Hierarchy. Saint Paul called this "the Christ in you, your hope of Glory" (*Colossians 1:27*).

- Christ is also the Splendour of God, the Cosmic Christ, the Cosmic Logos, the Original Word, through which and by which all things are made.

These three are one. This is the Mystery of the Christ.

Christ-Consciousness

Christ-Consciousness is Light-Consciousness. The Light of Christ, the Light of the World, dwells on the Buddhic Plane and descends onto the Astral Plane and hence into the Heart of the Mystic-Disciple. Christ-Consciousness is Intelligent Love, the human element combined with the Divine. This is the Mystery of the Christ.

CIDĀKĀŚA

Sanskrit: "The Self-Luminous Sky of Consciousness". The Infinite Space or Field of Universal Consciousness. The Boundless Ocean of Intelligence. The Wisdom- Mind which sees all things from above, from the point of view of the Transcendental Reality. CIDĀKĀŚA is ŚRĪ JAGADAMBĀ, the Holy World Mother. From this Pure Consciousness come forth all things, and all things dwell in Her and are maintained by Her.

Clairvoyance

From the French: "The ability to see clearly". The full usage of the astral and etheric sight and, in its higher aspects, the faculty of Spiritual Sight. True clairvoyance is extremely rare. True clairvoyance is the opening of the Third-Eye Cakra, the ŚIVANETRA, the Eye of Śiva, the All-Seeing Eye, the Eye of Wisdom. The true clairvoyance of the Third-Eye is direct vision, as clear and unimpeded as physical vision. The Egyptians called the visionary faculties *The Eye of Horus*. Clairvoyance has seven levels, the last of them being the Absolute or Beatific Vision.

Cosmic Consciousness

The term *Cosmic Consciousness* can be understood in two ways:

- The condition of absorption into the exalted Consciousness of NIRVĀṆA, the Kingdom of God (ĀTMĀ-VIDYĀ).
- The integration of the Buddhic Consciousness (Pure Consciousness, TURĪYA) into the states below. In this exalted condition, therefore, the objective consciousness, the subjective mind (dream states) and the dreamless-sleep state have fused perfectly into the Transcendental State of Pure Consciousness. One is simultaneously aware of the four states of Consciousness, from BUDDHI downwards, while functioning in the waking state in the physical body. This state is known as TURĪYĀTĪTA-AVASTHĀ, "beyond the Fourth State".

Creation

The Universe is a periodic, or cyclic, manifestation. During each period of manifestation, God creates in seven great Cosmic Days, seven vast periods of Cosmic Time, seven great Ages. Notice, God *creates*, because natural and supernatural Evolution are still going on and will go on for myriads of years of Earth-time. Thus: Science has to understand what Evolution really is, and religion has to understand what Creation really is, for they are the *same*.

Creative Hierarchies

The human prototype is but one of twelve Creative Hierarchies of intelligent entities which inhabit appropriate planets, realms and planes of our Solar System. Each of these Hierarchies consists of countless entities. The Hierarchies are groups of lives, at various stages of unfoldment and growth, who use vehicles of expression (forms or vestures), the vehicles varying according to the spiritual development reached.

Crown Centre

The Energy Centre at the top of the head, also called the *Thousand-Petalled Lotus*. The Crown Centre is wholly spiritual. It will put you in touch with the spiritual dimensions and, ultimately, with Nirvāṇa.

DEVĀCHAN

Tibetan: "The abode of the Shining Ones". The Shining Worlds. The *Seven Heavens*, the seven subplanes of the Mental Plane. The word sometimes refers to just the Causal Worlds, the three higher (formless) subplanes of the Mental Plane. In Sanskrit, DEVASTHĀNA.

DEVATĀ

Sanskrit: The Shining Divinity, Fiery-Light, the Shining Fire-God, the Spiritual-Sun. Also, a god or goddess. Non-human evolutionary orders or hierarchies. The Angelic Kingdoms. Angelic species everywhere, as distinct from the humanoid species (MANUṢYA).

Devil

Symbolically, the personality, which opposes the Spirit or Individuality. From the Greek DIABOLOS (an enemy, an accuser, a slanderer). It is true that there are evil spirits in the Universe, fallen angels and fallen human spirits in and around our planet. But no being is equal to God, so there cannot be an entity (called "the Devil") equal and opposite to God. The "devils" (fallen spirits) came *after* the Fall. (Note that there is no such thing as the horned and hoofed monster, so popular with some Christians.)

DHARMA

Sanskrit: "That which upholds all things". The Force of Destiny. From the Sanskrit root DHRI, "to support, uphold, maintain, carry on, preserve, bear, nourish, foster". Truth, the Ultimate Reality, Justice, Law, Virtue. In the old Sanskrit understanding, DHARMA means the Path that you should follow to become what you are *meant* to be.

Ēgō

Latin: "I" or "I am" (EGO-SUM). The original meaning is the Absolute Spiritual Self or "I AM", the MONAD (Greek), the SPIRITUS (Latin), the Divinity in Man. Later on, it also came to mean the Soul, the ANIMĀ (Latin), which is within the body and beyond the mind. Nowadays, the English word *ego* refers to the personal self, the PERSONA (Latin: the mask), the personality or body-conscious "I", the unreal "I", the false sense of self (the Sanskrit AHAṀKĀRA, "I am the doer").

Etheric Body

The etheric body exists on the etheric subplanes and is made up of the four states of etheric-physical matter. It is the vehicle of PRĀṆA, vitality, the Life-breath. It is also known as the *etheric-physical body*, the *subtle-physical body*, the *vital body* or the *etheric double*. In Sanskrit it is called LIṄGA-ŚARĪRA (symbolic body) because it is the prototype and Life-force of your dense physical body.

Etheric Web

An energy-structure within the etheric body which protects a physically embodied being from an influx of energies from the Inner Worlds. A human being has an etheric web, as does a planet and a solar system. At an advanced stage of human evolution the etheric web is burned away by the Kuṇḍalinī Fire, thus leading to Continuity of Consciousness and Cosmic Consciousness.

Evil

Evil means "physical imperfections and mind-created hell worlds". Evil is the wrong use of the One Force, Power, Energy or Substance (ŚAKTI) by living entities, whether through Ignorance or lack of Intelligence. Evil is caused by separative minds that do not feel and do not know the Unity of all Life. These evil minds can be human, subhuman (elemental) or angelic.

EVOLUTION

Latin: Unfolding, progression, metamorphosis, formation, growth, development, mutation, an unrolling, an opening up, a process of gradual, progressive change. There is a natural evolution (*horizontal* evolution) and there is a supernatural, spiritual evolution (*vertical* evolution). The scientific theory of natural evolution is correct but science hasn't even thought about the Supernatural Evolution.

Fall

The idea of "the Fall" can be understood on two levels:

- The descent of the Human Monads (Virgin Spirits) from the formless Causal Worlds into the material conditions of the Three Worlds, henceforth losing Awareness of the Immortal Luminous Oneness while cycling endlessly through the material realms (SAṀSĀRA). The Old Testament story of Adam and Eve being tempted by the serpent is symbolic of this event (the serpent being the KUṆḌALINĪ-ŚAKTI, the Evolutionary Force).

- The separation of a vast host of originally-luminous angels from the Primary State of Unity, millions of years ago, thus corrupting certain parts of the Omni-Revelation of the All-Mind. We cannot know whether the "fall" of these angels was by Cosmic Design or an act of free will. When the human family descended onto this planet it became caught up in the Cosmic Evil and has perpetuated it ever since.

Father

In Christianity, a symbol for the First Aspect of the Holy Trinity, the Eternal Cosmic Being, the First Logos. On a human level, the term "Father" or "Father in Heaven" symbolizes the MONAD, the Divine Spirit in Man (PARAMĀTMAN, the Transcendental Self, dwelling on the Paranirvāṇic Plane). In the New Testament the Eternal Cosmic Being is called "Father" due to the sexual bias of the old Jewish religious concepts.

GANDHARVA

Sanskrit: Music-Angel. This Sanskrit word is most esoteric. It refers to the Sound-Angels, the Celestial Angelic Musicians, the non-human (angelic) Intelligences which produce the sounds and colours in the Inner Worlds. The GANDHARVAs live by creating the most exquisite music, sound, tone, colour and harmony in the Astral World. They like events which include music, singing or dancing and often add their musical skills on the Astral to produce glorious effects.

GĀYATRĪ-MANTRA

Sanskrit: The most sacred Mantram of India. Also known as the SAVITĀ-Mantra, the SŪRYA-Mantra, the SAVITṚ-Mantra or ŚIVA-SŪRYA. This Mantra invokes the Male Aspect of the Solar Logos (the Solar Logos is Male-Female-Neuter, all at once). This is the Mantra for Enlightenment, Illumination, Transfiguration in Light, moving with the forces of evolution, progress, development. The GĀYATRĪ is a prayer, not a relaxation technique; it should never be repeated after a Haṭha Yoga class as a relaxation exercise.

God-Consciousness

The term *God-Consciousness* (BRAHMĀ-VIDYĀ) can refer to the following conditions:

- The State of Union with the Divine Being, the Monad, the "Father in Heaven" (PARAMĀTMAN). Also called *Divine-Consciousness.*

- The integration and fusing of the Nirvāṇic Consciousness (ĀTMĀ-VIDYĀ) into the states below.

GURU

Sanskrit: The Illuminator, the Dispeller of Darkness, the Bringer of Light, the Enlightener. The Transcendental Wisdom of God (BRAHMAN), of the Self (ĀTMAN), and of your physical Teacher or Preceptor. Sometimes called GURUDEVA (Divine Teacher) or SAT GURU (True Master). The Master or Spiritual Guide—the Guide of your Soul, not of your personality! Nowadays the word *guru* is commonly used by the ignorant to refer to a mentor or advisor, or any person who gives religious instructions, or an intellectual guide, or any leader or authority in any field. The original Sanskrit word GURU has only a deeply *religious-spiritual* meaning.

HAṬHA YOGA

Sanskrit: The best-known branch of Yoga in the West, HAṬHA Yoga consists of ĀSANAS (postures), PRĀṆĀYĀMAS (breath-controls), MUDRĀS (seals), BANDHAS (restraints) and ŚAT-KRIYĀS (purificatory exercises). It is sometimes called the "physical" Yoga, or the Yoga of the body, because it emphasizes the subjugation of the physical vehicle and the balancing of the "Sun" and "Moon" currents in the etheric body. Nowadays, Haṭha Yoga is thought to be nothing but keep-fit exercises. By the ancient definition, however, Haṭha Yoga has nothing at all to do with "keeping fit". Haṭha Yoga focuses on the *subjugation* of the physical body.

Heart

The Heart is *not* the heart in your physical body. It is a *psychic-spiritual* Heart located near the physical heart, in the subtler dimensions. There are three regions of the Heart:

- The *physical heart*, located in the physical body in this three-dimensional world.

- The *psychic Heart*, connected to your psychic being on the fourth-dimensional level of Space (the astral body).

- The *Spiritual Heart*, the centre of your true Self or Spirit, on the sixth-dimensional level of Space (Buddhi) and above.

The Mystics of Judaism, Christianity, Islam and Hinduism concentrate in the Heart to discover the Path that leads to "the Kingdom of God within"—the Higher Consciousness.

Heaven

In the language of the Old and New Testaments there is a shortage of words to describe Spiritual Realities. For instance, the word *Heaven* (or *Heavens*) is used to signify the sky, the starry space above, the after-death worlds, the Kingdom of God, and so on. *Heaven* is called SHEMAYĀ in Aramaic, SHAMAYĪM in Hebrew, OURANOS in Greek, CAELUM in Latin. In each of these Western languages which relate to original Christianity, *Heaven* means the multidimensionality of Space, as a Unity or Oneness, as a Continuum between the within (the above) and the without (the below).

Heaven Worlds

The *lower heavens* are the higher, subtler regions of the Astral World. These regions of the Astral World are more rarefied, artistic, intellectual, scientific, creative and religious than the regions below. People in this realm mistakenly call it "Heaven". The true *Heaven Worlds*, however, are the seven subplanes of the Mental Plane, known in the East as DEVA-STHĀNA, "the abode of the gods" (DEVĀCHAN in Tibetan), and in the Christian religion as the *Seven Heavens*.

Hell Worlds

The seventh subplane of the Astral Plane of this Earth-planet. This realm lies in the fourth dimension, partly on the surface of the physical Earth and partly below it, in the solid crust. The experience of "Hell", as described by thousands of people and by all world religions, is real. "Hell" is quite literally a product of the sufferer's mind, as is the "Heaven" of a more saintly person, because *mind* (whether human or angelic) creates the outer environment in which an entity lives.

Holy Spirit (Holy Ghost)

The Holy Breath, Holy Life-Force, Holy Intelligence, Holy Creative Power. The Radiant Creative Energy, the Fire of Creation. The Cosmic Fiery Energy of the Third Logos, the Third Person of the Trinity. The Holy Spirit is the Immanent Deity (BRAHMĀ, in Sanskrit), that which is concealed in matter, life-forms, bodies. It is God-in-Manifestation, the Embodied God. It is the Organizing and Structurizing Power within the Universe, God's Divine Mind at work, or Cosmic Intelligence. Also known as SHEKINAH (the Divine Presence) in Hebrew, and ŚAKTI (the Divine Energy) in Sanskrit.

ĪŚVARA

Sanskrit: "The Lord-God". The Master, Ruler, Controller, Director. The Supreme Being, the Cosmic Spirit, the Central Intelligence of the Universe, the Highest Authority in the Cosmos. The Lord of All, the Lord of the Universe, the Chief among All, the King of Kings, the Lord of Lords, the Master Power, the Inner-Ruler-Immortal. ĪŚVARA is the Heart Centre, or Centre of Consciousness, in any system, microcosmic or macrocosmic. It is the power of Lordship and independent action, the ruling, guiding or controlling principle within.

Jesus

The word *Jesus* comes from the Latin IESUS and IESU, which were derived from the older Greek IESOUS and the still older Hebrew and Aramaic YESHUA, YOSHUA, YEHESHUA, YEHOSHUA or YEHESHUVAH. As a Jewish child He probably would have been known as YOSHUA (JOSHUA). Like the peoples of India, the Jews gave Divine Names to their children. YEHESHUA means "the Eternal is my Salvation, in God is Salvation, God is my helper". YESHUA means "Saviour, Deliverer, Salvation, the Power to Save or Liberate, God's down-pouring Grace". Hence, *Jesus* means "the Saviour".

Jesus Christ

A compound of Hebrew and Greek words meaning "a Divine Teacher or Guru who has been anointed, or who has been acknowledged as succeeding in the Mysteries of Life and Death". The name "Jesus Christ" is correctly *Jesus the Christed One* (in the original Hebrew, YEHESHUAH HA-MASHIAH).

KALI YUGA

Sanskrit: "The Dark Age" (this is not a reference to the Dark Ages of European history). KALI YUGA is the Age of materialism, ignorance and darkness. We live in the Age of KALI YUGA. In this Age materialism prevails, spiritual ignorance and blindness, called MĀYĀ. The peoples of the Earth are blinded by material energies, material powers, material objects. The lives of people are taken up with accumulating material objects for themselves and their families. Material comforts supersede spiritual powers. Name and fame in society supersede the true Kingliness and Majesty of the Perfected Man.

KARMA

Sanskrit: "Action". Cause and effect, action and reaction, the effect or results of action. From the root KRĪ, "to do, to act, to perform". KARMA is the Law of Cause and Effect, the Universal Law governing all actions: past actions causing present events, and present actions causing future events. Every action has a corresponding reaction; that is, the reaction is *in kind*. In the Jewish, Christian and Muslim religions, karmas are called "sins"—transgressions against the Laws of Nature, which are the Laws of Mind. All actions are caused by some mind; therefore, Karma rules Mind. The Lord Buddha called it "the Good Law".

Kingdom of God

The expression *The Kingdom of God* can represent several things:

- The invisible Spiritual Hierarchy.
- Specifically, the Nirvāṇic Plane.
- Generally, all the invisible planes.

The flow of the great Revelation of the Kingdom of God presses downward from Nirvāṇa throughout the ages: down through the Buddhic Plane, the Causal Worlds, the Mental Plane and the Astral Plane, finally manifesting on the Physical Plane, in this Physical World.

Kīrtana

Sanskrit: Devotional singing and dancing. Devotional chanting, which stirs the Śabda, the God-Incarnating Sound. Also, Sankīrtana.

Lemuria

The third great epoch, or Root-Race, of human evolution upon this planet, preceding Atlantis. The Lemurian epoch concerned itself with the Physical Plane, with the evolution of the gross physical body and the two lowest cakras—the Base Cakra and the Sex Cakra. The physical body of Man has since been slowly evolving over countless millennia. The Lemurian epoch led to gross magic, black magic, earth-control, and so forth. During this epoch, people could not "feel".

Liberation

The Freedom of the Soul from birth and death in the lower worlds (Saṁsāra, wandering). Freeing your consciousness from the pains, delusions and errors of the lower worlds and experiencing the realms of Buddhi and Nirvāṇa. Being able to live freely in the Spirit, unhindered by your physical body, mind and personality structure. Conscious Immortality. In the West this is known as *Salvation* and *Beatitude*. In Sanskrit, Mokṣa (Freedom) and Mukti (Liberation).

Light

Light is not a metaphor or a symbol. It is real. In fact, it is the only Reality! Light is God-in-Manifestation, God-in-Incarnation, God-in-Expression. Light is God's Presence in Creation. Light is living, conscious, substantial Intelligence. Your Soul is made out of It. The physical light of the Sun, Moon and stars is but a fragment of Light. Light is Substance, Matter of a higher order, many invisible grades of Substance and Essence. Light is many-layered, multi-dimensional. The Light may be found in the Heart Centre, in the Third-Eye Centre and in the Crown Centre. Light is a Field of Energy emanated by God. When you see the Inner Light, you are *close* to God.

Limbo

The *limbo* states are states in the etheric-physical body on the subtle levels of the Physical Plane. This is the realm of the "ghosts", the earthbound spirits. Sometimes this term refers to the purgatory conditions of the Astral World.

Living Soul

Sanskrit: The Human Soul, dwelling on the formless subplanes of the Mental Plane and reflecting the triune nature of the Universal Being as ĀTMA-BUDDHI-MANAS. The Living Soul is below the Spiritual Soul (BUDDHI), which is in turn below the Spiritual Self (ĀTMAN). Called JĪVA or JĪVĀTMAN in Sanskrit, PSYCHE in Greek, NAFS in Arabic. In the East it is called the *Thinker* and the *Reincarnating Ego* because it takes on a new personality with each new incarnation. When functioning through the personality it is known as AHAṀKĀRA, "I am the doer". This is the personality's sense of "I am".

Logos

Greek: To the Greek Mystery Schools, the LOGOS was the Creative Word of God, the Universal Creative Intelligence, the Wisdom of God as a *Power*, the Source of Creation, the Cosmic Fatherhood, the Source of all things, the Creative God who created the Universe and in whom the Universe exists (Cosmic Logos), or who created the Solar System (Solar Logos). The Christians borrowed this idea from the Greeks: the LOGOS is the "Word" of the Christian Bible. The Christian fathers adapted the LOGOS doctrine to Christianity as follows: the *Father* is the First Logos; the *Son* (or Christ) is the Second Logos; and the *Holy Spirit* is the Third Logos. Yet there is only One God (One Cosmic LOGOS).

Love

Love is an Energy. It is not just a thought or a nice idea. It is a Force, a Power.

- There is personality Love.
- There is Soul Love (Group Love).
- There is Divine Love (Cosmic Love).

Love is not sex. The sexual energy is astral-etheric. In a human being the Energy of Love is found in the Heart Centre.

Lower Mind

The rational mind or concrete mind. In Sanskrit, RŪPA-MANAS (form-mind). It is the activity of the mental body (MĀNASA-RŪPA), functioning on the lower (form) levels of the Mental Plane. This is the common mind, the ordinary intellect, which is connected to the region of the brain between the physical eyes. Most people nowadays are stuck in the brain-mind due to the influence of their upbringing and the worldly education system.

MAITREYA

Sanskrit: "The Compassionate One". Friendly, compassionate, benevolent. It was the Lord Christ, ĪŚA-MAITREYA, who overshadowed that Great Master who was called JOSHUA (Jesus). MAITREYA is the World Teacher, the Teacher of Angels and Man, who is responsible for the spiritual development of the Angelic species and Mankind upon this planet. MAITREYA looks after all religious development upon this planet through His agents, the Spiritual Teachers, Saints, Yogīs, Adepts and Mystics, in all religions (Christianity being but one of them). MAITREYA is the Heart of the Spiritual Hierarchy of our planet.

Man

Man is an old English (Teutonic) word, synonymous with the Latin HOMO and the Hebrew ADAM, which means "a human being, a human creature", as distinct from the Animal, Vegetable or Angelic Kingdoms. The word *Man* refers to the human species, the genus of the human race, of both male and female genders. It does not mean only males. *Man* or *Mankind* is "the two-legged species with the thinking brain." Esoterically, *Man* is that Being in the Universe in which the highest Spirit (the Monad) is conjoined to the lowest matter (the physical body) by the Intelligent Principle (the mind). In Sanskrit, MANUṢYA or NARA.

MANAS

Sanskrit: Mind. The ruling, regulating, creative, ordering principle. The intelligent purpose of some being, working out into active objectivity. In Man, the principle of MANAS has two aspects:

- Higher Mind, KĀRAṆA-MANAS (Causal Mind), which is abstract and formless.
- Lower mind, RŪPA-MANAS (form-mind). The lower mind is usually tinged with desire, thus producing KĀMA-MANAS (desire-mind).

MANTRA, MANTRAM

Sanskrit: "An instrument of the mind, a thinking-tool, an instrument of thought, a mental creation, a thought-vibration". From MANAS (mind) and TRA (a tool or instrument). TRA also means "to transcend" and "to protect". Thus, a Mantra is an instrument of your mind, it protects your mind, and it also helps you to transcend the mind. Mantra is most often identified with *sound*.

A Mantra is a sound-formula outwardly chanted, intoned or sung, or inwardly spoken, sung and *realized*. Mantras, in Sanskrit, Hebrew, Arabic, Greek, Latin and Chinese, are energy-units to stimulate your Higher Evolution and your Transformation into the likeness of the God-Being within you.

Materialism

The belief in objective matter existing on its own, without the Being of God. The false view that physical matter is all that constitutes the Universe, that mind, Soul and Spirit are but material activities (the brain, nervous system, etc.). Materialists do not have open minds. Their minds are blocked by the false assumption that what they can sense with their physical senses is all that exists. Both orthodox religion and orthodox science are produced by the personality and serve the false, limited sense of ego or "I", the personality sense. They are the limited personality's view of Reality, not Reality as it really is, beyond the five senses.

MEDITATION

Latin: Originally, the Latin word MEDITATION meant "to contemplate Reality, to focus on Reality". This original meaning is radically different from the current usage of the word; only in later times has it come to mean "to think, to reflect, to ponder over a problem". Meditation is a search for Reality. Because Reality is not understood, however, meditation is not understood. This New Age of Aquarius is an extremely materialistic age; therefore, even meditation has been twisted into a quest for material progress. As defined in Mysticism, meditation is "a quiescent, prolonged, spiritual introspection; a devout religious exercise". Meditation is a quest for the Real, the Imperishable, the Eternal One.

Mediumship
Contacting the dead or one's "spirit-guides", the so-called "angelic beings", "masters" or "space brothers". Ordinary mediums (nowadays called "channellers") receive their messages from their own subconscious minds, or by allowing a spook on the Astral Plane to speak through them or use their etheric voice-box mechanism, which requires that energy (ectoplasma) be drawn from the etheric body of the medium and those in the seance or circle. Mediumship destroys your Soul's evolution because it locks your consciousness into the Astral World.

Mental Body
The vehicle of the lower mind, the concrete mind, the lower MANAS, existing on the lower four subplanes of the Mental Plane (those with form). In Sanskrit, MĀNASA-RŪPA or MANO-RŪPA (mind-form). The mental body is also called the MĀYĀVI-RŪPA (illusory form), because in those dimensions everything is but thoughtforms which, though illusory, appear very real to the perceiver.

Mental Plane
The fifth of the seven great Planes of Being (counting from above). As the name implies, the Mental Plane is a world of *mind*. The lower four mental subplanes are the realm of the *concrete* mind or *rational* mind, which shapes mental matter into *thoughtforms*. The higher three subplanes (the Causal Worlds) are *formless* and correspond with the *Higher Mind* or *Abstract Mind*. The Human Soul (JĪVA) dwells on the formless levels of the Mental Plane. The seven subplanes of the Mental Plane are the true *Heaven Worlds*. DEVĀCHAN in Tibetan. SVARGA, SUVAH-LOKA and DEVASTHĀNA in Sanskrit.

Mind
From the Latin MENS, MENTIS. The word *mental* comes from the Latin MENTALIS. The ordinary human mind is *above* the physical body experience and *above* the astral, which is psychic and emotional, having to do with feelings. Your normal "thinking mind" is your mental body, which exists on the Mental Plane separately from your physical body. It is an organism *independent* of the physical body and brain. Thus, when you are not in the physical body, you can use your "mind" as a body in order to function independently in the Mental World. In the Esoteric Teachings, however, the word *mind* does not refer to just the little mind of a member of the human species, but the minds of angels, gods and demigods, as well as Cosmic Intelligences and the Great Cosmic Mind of the Creator-God Him/Herself.

MOKṢA

Sanskrit: Freedom, Liberation, Salvation. The Freedom of the Soul from birth and death in the lower worlds. The State of Everlasting Bliss above the Heaven Worlds. Also called MUKTI (Liberation).

MONAD

Greek: "The Indivisible One". The Whole, the All, the Complete, the One. The Greek word MONAD means the same as the Latin ATOM (primordial unit) and the ancient classical Sanskrit AṆU. A MONAD, ATOM, AṆU, can be the little world known by science as the "atom" or it can be a human being, a planet, a solar system or a galaxy; they are all atoms of various sizes. In relation to Humanity, the MONAD is the Transcendental Spirit in Man, your "Father in Heaven", the I AM Presence in the innermost depths of the Soul (PARAMĀTMAN, in Sanskrit). It is the God-Self, the highest point of Spirit within Man, dwelling on the Paranirvāṇic Plane.

Mystery Schools

The Mystery Schools were created in ancient Egypt, Greece and Rome to link up the lower to the higher, the visible to the invisible worlds. In the Mystery Schools one learnt about the invisible worlds surrounding us and penetrating us, and the meditational practices or Path by which one climbs up the worlds into the purely spiritual dimensions, BUDDHI and NIRVĀṆA, the Kingdom of God.

NĀDA

Sanskrit: "The Soundless Sound". The Inner Sound. The Voice of the Silence. The Divine Word on the highest Spiritual Planes. The Pure Transcendental Sound of Absolute Reality. NĀDA is the Word of the Spirit, the First Aspect of the Deity. It is the Originating-Sounding-Light-Vibration, the Source, Silence.

Name

The *Name* is the Power emanated from *within* God, from Universal Consciousness. The Greek Mystics and Mystery Schools called this Power the LOGOS (the Word). The ancient Persians called it SRAOSHA (the Word or Name-Power). In ancient India is was called ŚABDA (the Living Word or Sound-Current) and NĀMA (the Name of God). It is as real as electricity, magnetism or atomic power—in fact, infinitely more so! It is invisible to physical eyes and permeates all of infinite Space and all the worlds, visible and invisible. The Name can be heard within the Heart as sweet Heavenly Music, and in the Head as the Cosmic-Ocean of Creative-Rumbling Word or Power, the Ocean-Tide of Life. Since very ancient times, the Mystics of all religions have called it by many Names, or expressions in human languages. These are known as the *Names of God* or *Divine Names*.

Nature

The word "Nature" does not just refer to what you behold with your physical eyes, for that is but an infinitesimal portion of the real Nature, the real Universe in which you "live, move and have your being". In Sanskrit, Nature is known as PRĀKṚTĪ, the matter or substance of all seven Planes of Being.

NIRMĀNAKĀYA

Sanskrit: The "Transformation Body" of a Buddha. A Buddha or Enlightened Being who remains in the Inner Worlds helping human evolution on all levels. These are the Saints, Yogīs and Masters of all religions who have attained Nirvāṇa but chose not to become absorbed in It (NIRVĀṆA-KĀYA). The NIRMĀNAKĀYAS are also known as BODHISATTVAS (those whose Essence is Love-Wisdom). Their Consciousness is focused in the Buddhic Plane, below Nirvāṇa. The NIRMĀNAKĀYAS have renounced Nirvāṇa in order to serve Humanity in the Inner Worlds, as far down as the Astral World. They are undying and Consciously Immortal, just like the NIRVĀṆĪS.

NIRVĀṆA

Sanskrit: Literally, "blown out, extinguished", from NIR (out, away from) and VĀṆA (to blow, to move). Commonly translated as "annihilation, destruction, dissolution". NIRVĀṆA is the blowing away of nescience, ignorance, darkness (MĀYĀ). NIRVĀṆA is Unconditioned Being, the annihilation of the personality in a Superior Consciousness, the cessation of Time, Space, form, matter and energy as we know them. In NIRVĀṆA one becomes One with the Universal "I AM", the Bright Self of the Universe.

ŌṀ

Sanskrit: The Word of Glory, the PRAṆAVA (Fundamental-Sound-Vibration of the Universe). Ōṁ is the Divine Word for Evolution, moving upwards and forwards and out of the Three Realms. Ōṁ is the Cosmic Word, the Logos, in the process of *ascending*, moving out of the Sphere of Creation-Activity. Ōṁ is the Sound of Purification and Union, Liberation and Resurrection, the Second Aspect of the Deity, the Christ Aspect or Power, the Sounding-Light Vibration which releases you from bondage to your forms and bodies. Ōṁ is the Formless-Self, the Sea of Pure Consciousness, Formless Awareness. Ōṁ is the Word of the Soul.

Omnipotent

From the Latin OMNI and POTENS: Infinite in power, unlimited in authority. All-powerful, mighty, supreme. A description of the Godhead.

Omnipresent

From the Latin OMNI and PRAESENS: Being present everywhere at the same time. Ubiquitous. A description of the Godhead. God is the all-enveloping Divine Law and Reality.

Omniscient

From the Latin OMNI and SCIENS: Having unlimited knowledge and understanding. The power to perceive and comprehend all things at once. A description of the Godhead.

PARABRAHMAN

Sanskrit: "Beyond Brahman". The Supreme Creative Intelligence. The One God. The Transcendental Reality. The Supreme Godhead. The Absolute Beingness. The Godhead beyond and above the Creator (BRAHMĀ). The Unknowable Absolute, which is limitless and which spreads Itself through endless Space. When in Creation, this Unmanifest Godhood forms a Veil upon Itself (MŪLAPRĀKṚTĪ) which conceals It from the sight of all created beings.

Personality

The lower self. From the Latin PERSONA. In the old Roman days, a PERSONA was a mask an actor wore for a particular act or play. Thus, the personality is but a mask over the Soul. The Soul is immortal, the personality is not. At death the Soul gradually removes the personality or mask it has worn for that lifetime (the physical, etheric, astral and mental bodies). Personality means acting, pretending, role-playing, which people do so seriously!

Physical Plane

The seventh and last of the seven great Planes of Being. In Sanskrit, PṚTHIVĪ-LOKA or BHŪR-LOKA. The lower three subplanes of the Physical Plane are called the *dense* or *gross* physical subplanes, corresponding to the three states of matter that we observe with our physical senses: solids, liquids and gases. The higher four subplanes are called the *etheric* or *etheric-physical* dimensions. Science is beginning to explore the etheric dimensions, without understanding them as such.

Piscean Age

The zodiacal period of approximately 2,150 years, preceding the Aquarian Age. The Piscean Age is presently drawing to a close. The Stream of Energy that was predominant during the Piscean Age (the Sixth Ray) produced in Human Consciousness the phenomenon of intense *idealism*. The orientation of the Piscean Age was towards the Soul and the invisible worlds and Realities, towards "God" (howsoever people understood that word).

Planes of Being
The seven great Planes of Being are seven states of MAHAT-PRĀKṚTĪ (Cosmic Nature, the Cosmic Physical Plane). The Planes of Being are realms, worlds or conditions of existence. Each of the seven great Planes of Being, the seven dimensions of our Universe, occupies the one Space. The Space is the same, but the *dimensions* are different, the *densities of matter* are different, and the *consciousness* is different in each of the strata of Creation. The matter or substance of each plane *interpenetrates* the one below it, which is of lower vibration and greater density.

Planetary Logos
A "Heavenly Man" which incarnates through the vehicle of a planet. One of the Cosmic Creators.

PRĀṆA
Sanskrit: "Breath, Life-breath, Life-force, Vitality, Energy, Fire". PRĀṆA is the Universal Life-Force Fire, the Energy of the Universe which flows through all things. It is a spiritual and psychic Energy which becomes the five Elements and gives *substance* to all objects. PRĀṆA, the invisible Life-Force, permeates all the seven great planes of the Solar System from *within*. PRĀṆA is the Breath of Life, the Breath of God, the Universal Life-Force that energizes Creation.

PRĀṆĀYĀMA
Sanskrit: "Control of the Life-breath". From PRĀṆA (the Life-force, the Life-breath) and YĀMA (to regulate, to control, to guide). Conscious breathing. Regulation of the vital-force or PRĀṆA, the Breath of Life. PRĀṆĀYĀMA also means PRĀṆA-AYĀMA (no-control, spontaneous, natural). Thus, esoterically, PRĀṆĀYĀMA means breath which is natural, not forced, in balance, equilibrated. True PRĀṆĀYĀMA occurs when the in-breathing and the out-breathing are naturally suspended (transcended) and one attains the tranquil state of breath (PRĀṆAVĀYU), which produces the tranquil mind, SAMĀDHI. When your breathing is calm and steady, your mind is calm and steady. When your mind is calm and steady, your breathing is calm and steady.

Pratyeka Buddha

Sanskrit: "An Enlightened One who walks alone". From Buddha (Enlightened One) and Pratyeka (alone). A Solitary Buddha. A fully enlightened Buddha who, having attained Nirvāṇic Consciousness, merges into Nirvāṇa, never to return to the lower realms. The Pratyeka Buddha has moved out of the human evolutionary field altogether and is therefore no longer accessible to Humanity on this planet.

Prophetes

Greek: Someone who knows the Will of God, the *Plan*, through an interior revelation, by direct experience. One who speaks for God, the Deity. An inspired *revealer* or *interpreter* of the Divine Will, the Divine Plan. From the Greek Prophecein, "to give religious instruction". From this came the English word *prophet*. A Prophet, in the Old Testament sense, and to the early Christians, was one who could speak on behalf of the Deity. Prophets were not confined to Israel only. Before Christianity, the Greeks and the ancient nations had many "prophets". The word, as used by them, had many distinct meanings.

Purgatory

The third, fourth and fifth subplanes of the Astral Plane, which appear to its denizens as very similar to the physical Earth. This is where ordinary people live after death. These people could be considered "earthbound" because their lives are a reflection of Physical Plane conditions and habits. For this reason these realms are sometimes called the *Reflection Sphere*.

Religion

From the Latin Re-ligare: "To tie, to fasten, to re-unite, to bind, to bring back". In the classical days of Rome, religion was an experience of Unity with the Divine, with the Godhead. Since the fourth century AD the word *religion* has been changed by the church to mean "a set of beliefs concerning the nature of the Universe and God; a set of fundamental (fundamentalist) beliefs and practices agreed upon by the church authorities; the practice of religious beliefs (dogmas), rituals and observances; faith, devotion, ritual, religious conviction".

Śabdabrahman (Śabda-Brahman)

Sanskrit: "The Sounding-God". The Sounding-Absolute. God Incarnate as the Eternal Word or Sound-Vibration. God as the Logos, Daiviprākṛtī, heard in deep meditation. The Incarnating Sound from which crystallizes the lower realms and worlds of Creation. All differentiations are caused by Śabda-Brahman. In each world, realm or region of the

Universe, ŚABDA creates a different Vibration. Thus, on each plane of the Solar System, ŚABDA (Sounding-Light-Consciousness) arranges things differently. All forms, no matter how gross or subtle, are constructed by Sound-Vibration.

SĀDHANĀ

Sanskrit: The Spiritual Life. Spiritual practice, spiritual discipline, quest. A Way or Path of Meditation consisting of the purification of the mind and the Heart, which results in the Union of the personal self with the Universal Self or ĀTMAN.

SĀDHU

Sanskrit: A good man, a virtuous man. A virtuous Saint who is a renunciate. A peculiarity of the sādhus and sannyāsins of India, and many yogīs, is their total lack of concern for their physical bodies and surroundings. This is caused by the shifting of the attention from personality-life into the Soul-life. Many of them exhibit abnormalities which Western psychology would classify as mental illness or psychotic behaviour. The aim of spiritual development, however, is to integrate or *synthesize* the human being so that he or she will become physical, imaginative, mental, intuitive and spiritual at the same time.

Saint

A true Saint is one who has attained Buddhic Consciousness or Nirvāṇic Consciousness. While a few of the Christian Saints were true Saints who entered the Kingdom of God, many were merely religious fanatics who converted people to the church, either by persuasion or by the sword. They were canonized by the popes because they converted people to the church, but they had no Higher Consciousness of any type. Furthermore, many *true* Saints were never recognized by the church. The church has always been totally confused about the true nature of a Saint.

ŚAKTI

Sanskrit: "Energy, force, power, strength, might, ability, skill". The Divine Energy. God's Dynamic Energy. The Holy Spirit. ŚAKTI is the Feminine side of the Deity. ŚAKTI is the totality of the *real* Energy and Forces of this Universe, on all layers and levels, on all planes of Existence. She is the Goddess in all Her many forms, aspects and manifestations, and She is the Universal Mother, both as all forms and as the Life *within* forms. All the powers of the various Goddesses are but expressions of ŚAKTI. All that Is is Energy (ŚAKTI).

SAMĀDHI

Sanskrit: "The collecting together of the Intuitive or Direct Awareness of Reality", from SAMA (together) and DHĪ (the faculty of Intuition, the inner realizing principle). Equilibrated-mind (SAMĀ-DHI). The state of equilibrium, tranquil knowing, intuitive perception, passive awareness. That stage of DHYĀNA (meditation) wherein the mind is no longer disturbed by anything. The mystical trance-state, the suspended animation of your ordinary mind. The no-mind state wherein the ordinary mind of reason and logic does not function and you experience Causal Consciousness and Pure Consciousness.

SAMSĀRA

Sanskrit: "Wandering" in the Three Worlds. Conditioned existence. Going around the Wheel of Birth and Death in the Three Worlds (the Physical, Astral and Mental Planes). SAMSĀRA, our material Creation, essentially represents a realm of woe and unsatisfactory existence.

SAMSKĀRA (SANSKĀRA)

Sanskrit: Previous subliminal (subconscious) impressions, or psychic imprints left over from previous embodiments. Mental behaviour resulting from past-life experiences and from previous experiences in this lifetime. Conditioning factors which give you your present moral and behavioural tendencies. Unconscious attachments to past habit patterns. The force of habits from the past. The karmic consequences of your past behavioural tenden-cies. SAMSKĀRA are accumulations of latent impressions from the past which will work out now or in the future. From SAMS (together) and KARA (acting, putting, doing). Impressions or grooves in the mental and astral bodies are "put together" from past thoughts, feelings and actions, which are the seeds for future Karma and Dharma. SAMSKĀRA are produced by external circumstances, and by thoughts, feelings and physical actions, which form seeds for actions, propensities or impulses in this or future lifetimes.

SANAT KUMĀRA

Sanskrit: The Lord of the World, the Ancient of Days, the King of Kings, the Lord of Lords, the Master of Masters on this planet. SANAT KUMĀRA is the Undying Seed of Eternal Life, the Youth of Endless Summers, the Eternally Undying One.

Self-Realization

Realization of the Self (the Soul) and the SELF (the Spirit). In Sanskrit, ĀTMĀ-VIDYĀ, ĀTMĀ-JÑĀNA, ĀTMĀ-BODHA.

Seven Heavens

The seven subplanes (regions, vibratory states, dwelling places) of the Mental Plane, or DEVĀCHAN. These are the true Heavens, beyond the lower heavens of the Astral World.

Shaman

The word *shaman* is a degeneration of the original Sanskrit word ŚRAMANA (an ascetic training for spiritual powers). A shaman is a witch-doctor of the American Indians, the Eskimos, the Tibetans and the Mongolians. All are descendents of the old Atlanteans.

SHEKINAH

Hebrew: "Radiating Light, Glory as Light Emanation". The Divine Fiery Energy. God's Immanence. The Cloud of Glory or Brightness within Creation. The Glory of God's Presence, illuminating the world from within. The Glorious Hebrew Name SHEKINAH means the Light of NIRVĀNA sent forth from the Infinite Light, AIN SOPH AUR. It is the Divine Presence in the Universe of Light, which is Feminine in nature towards the Boundless Godhead or Everlasting Light.

Solar Logos

A Cosmic Creator-God, such as our Sun. The physical body of our Solar Logos is our Solar System, and each planet is one of His cakras or "wheels of force". Many thousands of years ago these Creator-Gods (whose bodies are stars and planets) were called PRAJĀPATIS in India, DEMIURGOS and KOSMOKRATORES in old Greece, and ELOHĪM among the Semitic races of the Middle East.

Solar Plexus Centre

The Energy Centre which is responsible for your emotional well-being. All of your emotions, moods, feelings and desires go through it. It puts you in touch with the Astral World.

Spirit

The term *spirit* is often erroneously applied to disembodied beings on the Astral World, three planes below the realm of the true Human Spirit, ĀTMAN, the Self, dwelling on the Nirvānic Plane. The words *spirit* and *spiritual* come from the Latin SPIRITUS, which refers to both the Transcendent and Immanent aspects of God. The mediums degenerated the truth about *Spirit* and lowered it to astral phenomena.

Spiritual Hierarchy

Man's spiritual unfoldment is guided by the Planetary Hierarchy, the Great White Brotherhood, the Inner Government of the World, the Brotherhood of Light. It is also known as the Fifth Kingdom, the Kingdom of God, the Spiritual Kingdom, or the Christ-Hierarchy. It is the next human Hierarchy *above* the Human Hierarchy (the Fourth Kingdom). It is the Hierarchy of Saints, Masters, Yogīs and Teachers who have gone beyond the ordinary Man-type and are now evolving on the Causal, Buddhic and Nirvāṇic Planes. It is from these realms that the Hierarchy sends down AVATĀRAs, Divine Incarnations or Divine Messengers, to remind human beings of who they truly are, and to teach Mankind about the Kingdom of God. In Sanskrit, SAṄGHA or SATA-SAṄGHA.

Subconscious Mind

That which is *below* your conscious mind. The subjective mind, the dreaming mind, the symbolic mind. Dreamtime, imagination. The astral-body consciousness. In Sanskrit, SVAPNĀ-AVASTHĀ.

Subplane

Each of the seven great Planes of Being has seven subdivisions or *subplanes*—seven realms, spheres or vibrational states of increasingly finer matter or energy. Thus, there are a total of forty-nine subplanes, or states of matter, within the Cosmic Physical Plane of our Solar System. In the Secret Doctrine, the Primeval Wisdom, these forty-nine states of matter are called the *forty-nine Fires*.

SŪFĪ

Arabic-Persian: "One who has purified the Heart". One who has attained Mystical Union with God. A Pure One. A Muslim Saint. The SŪFĪs are all those great Saints of the Muslim religion who have attained Union with God, or who have merged into the Eternal Light. A SŪFĪ is "Pure in Heart" (QALB-SALĪM, a Heart that is Perfect). In the State of Perfection you perceive nothing else but God in all things, and the Divine becomes the Centre of your life, the Heart throb of your Being. Your personal ego is dissolved in God, FANĀ'FI-LLĀH.

ŚŪNYATĀ (ŚŪNYA)

Sanskrit: "Emptiness". A formless condition. A Buddhist term for the Mystical Consciousness (Buddhi), which is characterized by Formlessness, No-Thingness, Clarity, Light. NIRVĀṆA they call MAHĀŚŪNYATĀ (the Great Emptiness). To confuse the issue, some schools use this word to mean non-existence or unreality. Others use this word to mean the sky or space.

TAO

Chinese: "The Great Absolute Ruler, the Heavenly-Master of Creation". TAO has been translated as "the One Truth or Reality underlying all Creation, the Single Principle of the Universe". Everything emerges out of TAO, develops and returns to its Source, which is TAO. TAO is the Essential Simplicity, which is the Source, Root and Origin of things, and at the same time, the Way, the Truth and the Life. It is the Manifest and Unmanifest Godhead all at once, in Oneness. TAO is the *Being* or *Essence* of all things, the *Source of Active Power* within all things, the *Force* or *Energy* behind all forms. Not originated by anything, it is the One Principle which is before all else. Thus, TAO cannot be talked about, but It can be *demonstrated* by Silence and Consciousness. Some people call TAO "God".

TAT

Sanskrit: "That". The Inconceivable Reality. The One Existence, the Final Truth, the Boundless Absolute, the Eternal Godhead. PARABRAHMAN (the Boundless All, the Absolute Godhead), PARABRAHM (the Infinite Invisible Existence). The final, inconceivable, indescribable Absolute Truth or Reality of the Godhead within Man and the Cosmos. The Spiritual Sun. The Unnameable.

THEOLOGIA

Greek: "God-Knowledge". The Science of God-Realization. From THEOS (God) and LOGOS (God as the Creative Principle, the Divine Word or Wisdom, the Divine Discourse or Reason). Hence the degenerated English word *theology*. In the early centuries of Christianity, theology was not just a set of intellectual ideas and dogmas as it is today. It was the *direct realization* of Divine Realities, the *inner perception* of the Spiritual Realms and Hierarchies through the processes of prayer, meditation and contemplation, the direct *realization* of God, deep within the Soul.

Third-Eye Centre

The Third-Eye is located between the eyes and is responsible for your ordinary mind, your mental body. It puts you in touch with the lower Mental Plane. When awakened, it becomes the seat of Spiritual Vision. It has been called the Wisdom-Eye, the Eye of Śiva, the All-Seeing Eye, the Single-Eye, the Spiritual Eye, the Clairvoyant Eye, and the Cyclopean Eye.

Thoughtform

A thought-structure existing in the mental body, built from matter of the lower mental subplanes. In Sanskrit, MANASI-JĀ, "things born from the mind". In your natural condition you are completely surrounded by your thoughtforms. Although you cannot see them with your physical eyes, your thoughts are objective, real, and you could see them if you had mental clairvoyance. These thoughtforms block your perception of Reality. When you drop your mental activity, you will come to know the Things that Are.

VĀSANĀ

Sanskrit: Desires for the future. Longings, unfulfilled hopes, desires, drives, urges and psychic impulses left over from previous lives. Subliminal imprints left over from the scars, seeds, pains, traumas, stresses or desires of previous lives, to be re-enacted in this life or future lives as subconscious drives. Habit-patterns acquired in previous existences which form the character of a child at birth, and which include all the subconscious cravings to which a man or woman is predisposed. [See SAṀSKĀRA]

Wisdom

Wisdom is called PRAJÑĀ or BODHI in Sanskrit, CHOCKMAH in Hebrew, SOPHIA in Greek, SAPIENTIA in Latin. In ancient times, these words did not mean being "worldly-wise", intellectual, or learned in our present sense, but the Knowledge that revealed the Path of Light. This is the mind-transcending, Truth-discerning Awareness of Pure Consciousness. It is pure Knowing, without words, without thoughts, without the mind.

YOGA

Sanskrit: "Joining together, yoking, aligning, linking, uniting, going into Oneness or Union". From YUGH, "to unite, join, put together, integrate". The State of Union. Union with the ĀTMAN. Union with God. YOGA also means "a method, an application of a principle, a means to an end, an arrangement, meditation, devotion". YOGA requires the control of the mind and the emotions. When the emotions and mind are tranquil, the breath (the Life-force, PRĀṆA) is harmonized and the Self (ĀTMA) is realized.

YOGA-NIDRĀ

Sanskrit: "The Sleep of the YOGĪ". This occurs when the Heart is awake and the rest of the human being is asleep. True YOGA-NIDRĀ is not falling off to sleep during meditation. In YOGA-NIDRĀ one's body and senses are at rest (asleep), while one's consciousness is wide awake inside.

Yogī, Yogin, Yoginī

Sanskrit: "One who is united or integrated". A practitioner of the Science of Yoga (YOGA-MĀRGA). One who has attained the State of Union (YOGA), or SAMĀDHI. Or, one who has attained the highest state of Yoga or Union (Nirvāṇic Consciousness). A Saint of the Hindu and Esoteric Buddhist religions who has attained Union with ĀTMAN (the Universal Spirit) and BRAHMAN (the Ultimate Reality). A female YOGĪ or YOGIN is called a YOGINĪ.

SANSKRIT PRONUNCIATION GUIDE

~

Vowels

A	AS IN FATHER
E	... THERE
I	... MACHINE
O	... GO
U	... FULL
R̥	... MERRILY (ROLLED)
R̥̄	... MARINE
AI	... AISLE
AU	... HAUS (GERMAN)

Long Vowels

Ā, Ī, Ū

THE LONG VOWELS ARE PRONOUNCED THE SAME AS THE SHORT VOWELS, BUT ARE OF LONGER DURATION (TWO OR THREE MEASURES). O AND E ARE ALWAYS SOUNDED LONG. THE LONG Ö INDICATES A PROLONGED SOUNDING.

Semi-Vowels

H	... HEAR
Y	... YET, LOYAL
R	... RED
V	... IVY
	... MORE LIKE W WHEN FOLLOWING A CONSONANT
L	... LULL

Guttural Consonants

SOUNDED IN THE THROAT.

K	... KEEP
KH	... INKHORN
G	... GET, DOG
GH	... LOGHUT
Ṅ	... SING (NASAL)

Palatal Consonants

SOUNDED AT THE ROOF OF THE MOUTH.

C	... CHURCH
CH	... CHAIN
J	... JUMP
JH	... HEDGEHOG
Ñ	... SEÑORITA

Cerebral Consonants

SOUNDED WITH THE TONGUE TURNED UP TO THE ROOF OF THE MOUTH.

Ṭ	... TRUE
ṬH	... ANTHILL
Ḍ	... DRUM
ḌH	... REDHAIRED
Ṇ	... NONE

SANSKRIT PRONUNCIATION GUIDE

~

DENTAL CONSONANTS

SOUNDED WITH THE TIP OF THE TONGUE AT
THE FRONT TEETH.

T	... WATER
TH	... NUTHOOK
D	... DICE
DH	... ADHERE
N	... NOT

LABIAL CONSONANTS

SOUNDED AT THE LIPS.

P	... PUT, SIP
PH	... UPHILL
B	... BEAR
BH	... ABHOR
M	... MAP, JAM

SIBILANTS

THE SIBILANTS ARE HISSING SOUNDS.

S	... SAINT
Ś	... SURE
Ṣ	... SHOULD, BUSH

NASAL SOUNDS

THE NASAL SOUNDS ARE SOUNDED AS A
HUMMING IN THE ROOT OF NOSE. THE
FOLLOWING REPRESENT INCREASING DEGREES
OF NASALIZATION:

M, Ṁ, Ṅ (NG), ṄG

ASPIRATED SOUNDS

H	ASPIRATED OUT-BREATHING
Ḥ	DEEPER OUT-BREATHING

VARIATIONS

THE VOWELS Ṛ AND Ṝ ARE SOMETIMES
WRITTEN AS ṚI, RI OR RĪ WHEN FALLING AT THE
END OF A WORD.
FOR EXAMPLE: SĀVITRĪ

SOME COMMON EXAMPLES OF ANGLICIZED
SPELLINGS

CAKRA	... 'CHAKRA'
ṚSI	... 'RISHI'
SVĀMĪ	... 'SWAMI'
ŚAKTI	... 'SHAKTI'
ĀKĀŚA	... 'AKASHA'
KRṢNA	... 'KRISHNA'
ĀŚRAMA	... 'ASHRAM'
AVATĀRA	... 'AVATAR'

ANGLICIZED SPELLINGS APPEAR IN
THIS WORK ONLY IN THE CONTEXT
OF POPULAR USAGE.

ABOUT THE AUTHOR

~

Born in 1940 in Budapest, Hungary, Imre Vallyon emigrated to New Zealand at the age of sixteen. After having many mystical experiences and inner revelations throughout his childhood, he reached Enlightenment at the age of nineteen and thereafter dedicated his life to teaching the Wisdom Science through his writings and through workshops and retreats held around the world.

Imre's extraordinary knowledge of human spirituality is neither derived from scholarly research nor channelled from the psychic dimensions. His writings issue forth spontaneously from his own Interior Realization of Higher Realms of Consciousness; therefore, they are salient messages of Truth for everyone today.

Imre's work is one of synthesis. His writing is universal, not biased towards any particular religion or tradition. His Teaching spans the full spectrum of human experience: reaching through time, illuminating the great Spiritual Teachings and Sacred Languages of our planetary history while pointing the way to the future. Over the past decade his writings and talks have been focused on the momentous changes our planet is undergoing and how Humanity can work with these new energies of change not only for personal Liberation but also for Planetary Transformation, the birth of a true Golden Age on Earth.

Imre presently lives near Hamilton, New Zealand, where he founded in 1980 the *Foundation for Higher Learning*, an international Spiritual School for the Soul with well-established centres in Europe, North America and Australasia. Following Imre's guidance and practising a wide array of meditation techniques, FHL members work to discover their own Soul Potential and contribute towards the raising of human consciousness, even as they strive to be *in* the world, but not *of* the world.

Imre Vallyon's four-volume treatise *Heavens & Hells of the Mind* won a gold medal in the 2009 Living Now Awards and was awarded first place in the prestigious Ashton Wylie Charitable Trust Awards.

SELECTED TITLES

~

Heavens & Hells of the Mind
ISBN 978-0-909038-30-4

The Magical Mind
ISBN 978-0-909038-11-8

The Warrior Code
ISBN 978-0-909038-64-9

Planetary Transformation
ISBN 978-0-909038-61-8

Know Your Own Mind
ISBN 978-0-9038-17-5

The Divine Plan
ISBN 978-0-909038-53-3

The Art of Meditation
ISBN 978-0-9038-56-4

Please refer to our catalogue for a full list of products.

Sounding-Light Publishing

FOR MORE INFORMATION
~

Americas
PO Box 14094
San Francisco
CA 94114-0094
United States of America

Asia-Pacific
PO Box 771
Hamilton 3240
New Zealand

Europe
PO Box 134
2000 AC Haarlem
The Netherlands

Online
www.planetary-transformation.org
www.soundinglight.com
info@soundinglight.com

CPSIA information can be obtained at www.ICGtesting.com
Printed in the USA
LVOW100740210113

316430LV00005B/12/P